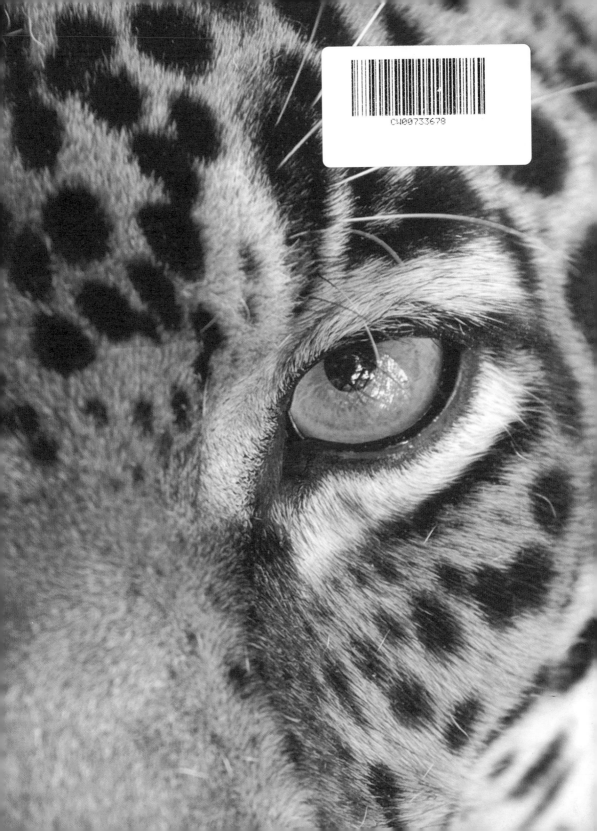

WILD ABOUT
FIERCE CREATURES

WILD ABOUT

FIERCE CREATURES

WRITTEN BY
CAMILLA DE LA BÉDOYÈRE,
STEVE PARKER, BARBARA TAYLOR

Miles
Kelly

First published in 2019 by Miles Kelly Publishing Ltd
Harding's Barn, Bardfield End Green, Thaxted, Essex, CM6 3PX, UK

Copyright © Miles Kelly Publishing Ltd 2019

This edition printed 2020

2 4 6 8 10 9 7 5 3 1

Publishing Director Belinda Gallagher
Creative Director Jo Cowan
Editorial Director Rosie Neave
Cover Designer Simon Lee
Designers Rob Hale, Joe Jones, Andrea Slane
Image Manager Liberty Newton
Production Elizabeth Collins, Jennifer Brunwin-Jones
Reprographics Stephan Davis
Assets Lorraine King

Consultants Camilla de la Bédoyère, Steve Parker, Barbara Taylor

ISBN 978-1-78989-162-1

Printed in China

British Library Cataloguing-in-Publication Data
A catalogue record for this book is available from the British Library

Made with paper from a sustainable forest

www.mileskelly.net

Contents

DEADLY CREATURES 6

Killer carnivores 8
Lethal weapons 10
Skills to kill 12
Canine killers 14
Ambush and attack 16
Mighty monsters 18
Dragons and monsters 20
Fearsome frogs 22
Eight-legged hunters 24
Clever defenders 26
Danger at sea 28
Sharks in the shadows 30
Peril at the shore 32
Minibeasts 34
The enemy within 36

VENOM 38

Why have venom? 40
Venom or poison? 42
Potent poisons 44
Warning displays 46
Venomous to who? 48
Types of venom 50
Delivering doses 52
Jelly killers 54
Venomous molluscs 56
Insect slayers 58

Dangerous spiders 60
Scorpions and centipedes 62
Stars and spines 64
Venomous fish 66
Lethal lizards 68
Mammal bites and spurs 70
Friends and enemies 72
Most deadly 74
Valuable venom 76

SNAKES 78

What is a snake? 80
Scaly skin 82
Colours and patterns 84
On the move 86
Super senses 88
Hunting and eating 90
Teeth and jaws 92
Poisonous snakes 94
Cobras and vipers 96
Crushing coils 98
Boas and pythons 100

BIRDS OF PREY 102

Eagle-eyed predators 104
Hovering and soaring 106
Hunting weapons 108
Fussy eaters 110

Snake stampers 112
Eagles 114
Kites and buzzards 116
Fast falcons 118
Hawks and harriers 120
Hunters of the night 122

BIG CATS 124

King of the jungle 126
Jaws and claws 128
Spotted sprinter 130
Sociable simba 132
American athlete 134
A coat to die for 136
Supercat 138

BEARS 140

What is a bear? 142
Habits and homes 144
Black bears 146
Polar bears 148
Brown bears 150
Gone hunting 152
Bear behaviour 154
Bear myths and legends 156

INDEX 158
ACKNOWLEDGEMENTS 160

DEADLY CREATURES

1 The world is full of animals that are fighting to survive. There are many reasons why animals may attack one another. Some are called predators and they kill for food. Others only kill to defend themselves, their young or their homes. Whatever the reason for using their claws, jaws, poisons or stings, these creatures are fascinating, but deadly.

▼ To catch its prey, the Nile crocodile lies very still in the water until the gazelle comes close. Then it shoots out of its hiding place, trying to catch the gazelle in its powerful jaws.

Killer carnivores

◀ False vampire bats have very sharp teeth, like the vampire bat. They catch and feed on frogs, mice, birds and other bats.

2 **Animals that eat meat are called carnivores.** Scavengers are carnivores that steal meat from others, or find dead animals to eat. Most carnivores, however, have to hunt and kill. These animals are called predators.

3 **Killer whales are some of the largest predators in the world.** Despite their size, these mighty beasts often hunt in groups called pods. By working together, killer whales can kill large animals, including other whales. However, they usually hunt smaller creatures, such as sea lions and dolphins.

▼ Anacondas are types of boa, and are the heaviest snakes in the world. As they don't have chewing teeth, snakes swallow their prey whole. Anacondas feed on large rodents called capybaras, deer, fish and birds.

4 **Vampire bats do not eat meat, but they do feed on other animals.** With their razor-sharp teeth, vampire bats pierce the skin of a sleeping animal, such as a horse or pig, and drink their blood. False vampire bats are bigger, and they eat the flesh of other animals.

5 With their cold eyes and gaping mouths, piranhas are fierce-looking predators. When a shoal, or group, of piranhas attack, they work together like an enormous slicing machine. Within minutes, they can strip a horse to its skeleton using their tiny triangular teeth.

▲ Red piranhas are aggressive, speedy predators. They work together in a group to attack their prey, such as birds.

6 Some snakes rely on venom, or poison, to kill their prey, but constrictors squeeze their victims to death. Pythons and boas wrap their enormous bodies around the victim. Every time the captured animal breathes out, the snake squeezes a little tighter, until its prey can no longer breathe.

Lethal weapons

7 **Many animals have deadly weapons, including teeth, claws, horns and stings.** They are perfect for killing prey, or fighting enemies.

8 Inside the mouth of a meat-eating predator is an impressive collection of deadly daggers – teeth. Different teeth do different jobs. Canines, or fangs, are long and knife-like, and are used to grab prey or pierce skin. Teeth at the front of the mouth are very sharp, and are ideal for cutting and slicing flesh.

◀ Mandrills are part of the same family as monkeys, called primates. Males bare their enormous fangs when they are anxious, or want to scare other males. The fangs may reach up to 7 centimetres in length.

9 Stings are common weapons in the animal world and they are used by creatures such as jellyfish and scorpions. Stings usually contain poison, or venom. The stingray, for example, is a fish with a long saw-shaped spine on its tail, which is coated in poison.

10 Elephant and walrus tusks are overgrown teeth that make fearsome weapons when used to stab and lunge at attackers. Males use their tusks to fight one another at mating time, or to scare away predators. An elephant can kill a person with a single thrust from its mighty tusks.

▼ Birds of prey grab hold of their victim with powerful talons, which pierce the flesh with ease.

▼ Cats have sharp claws that can be pulled back into the paws when they are not being used.

12 Some animals fight for mates, or territory (the area they live in). Horned animals, such as deer, are not predators, but they may fight and attack other animals. These animals have been known to harm humans when they are scared.

11 Eagles have huge claws called talons. The bird grasps prey in its feet, killing it by piercing and squeezing with its talons. Eagles and other carnivorous (meat-eating) birds are called birds of prey.

▲ Ibex are wild goats. They use their thick, curved horns to fight for mates or territory. Horns can be used to stab, wound and even kill.

Skills to kill

13 **Monkeys and apes belong to the same group of animals as humans, called primates.** These intelligent creatures have great skills of communication and teamwork. Although monkeys, gorillas and chimps appear to be playful, they can be dangerous.

14 **It was once believed that chimps only ate plants and insects.** However, it has been discovered that groups of chimps ambush and attack colobus monkeys. Each chimp takes its own role in the hunting team. During the chase, the chimps communicate with each other by screeching and hooting.

15 **Chimps also kill each other.** Groups of male chimps patrol the forest, looking for males from another area. If they find one, the group may gang up on the stranger and kill him.

▶ Chimps use their great intelligence to organize hunts. Some of them scream, hoot and chase the colobus monkey. Other chimps in the group hide, ready to attack.

16 **Baboons live in family groups and eat a wide range of foods, from seeds to antelopes.** Young males eventually leave their family, and fight with other males to join a new group and find mates.

17 A mighty gorilla may seem fierce, but it is actually one of the most gentle primates. Large adult males, called silverbacks, only charge to protect their families by scaring other animals, or humans, away. Gorillas can inflict terrible bite wounds with their fearsome fangs.

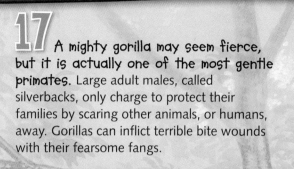

I DON'T BELIEVE IT!

Chimps are skilled at making and using tools. It is easy for them to hold sticks and rocks in their hands. They use sticks to break open insects' nests and they use rocks to smash nuts.

Canine killers

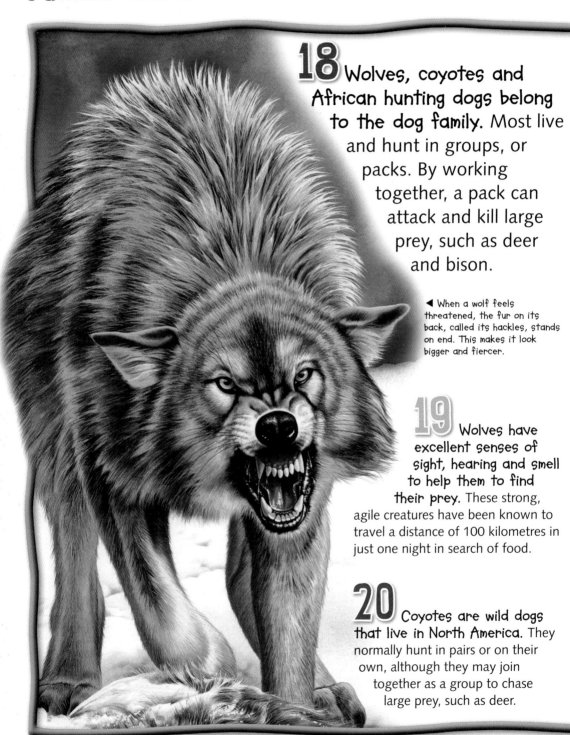

18 Wolves, coyotes and African hunting dogs belong to the dog family. Most live and hunt in groups, or packs. By working together, a pack can attack and kill large prey, such as deer and bison.

◄ When a wolf feels threatened, the fur on its back, called its hackles, stands on end. This makes it look bigger and fiercer.

19 Wolves have excellent senses of sight, hearing and smell to help them to find their prey. These strong, agile creatures have been known to travel a distance of 100 kilometres in just one night in search of food.

20 Coyotes are wild dogs that live in North America. They normally hunt in pairs or on their own, although they may join together as a group to chase large prey, such as deer.

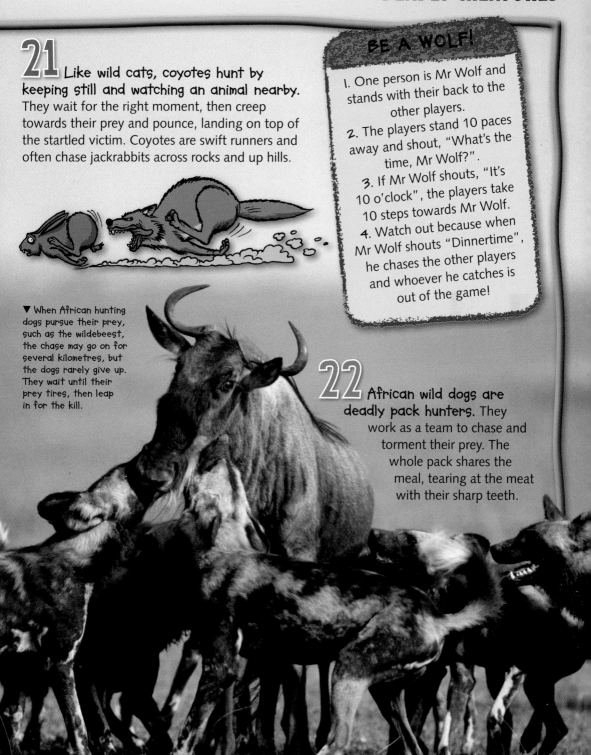

21 Like wild cats, coyotes hunt by keeping still and watching an animal nearby. They wait for the right moment, then creep towards their prey and pounce, landing on top of the startled victim. Coyotes are swift runners and often chase jackrabbits across rocks and up hills.

BE A WOLF!

1. One person is Mr Wolf and stands with their back to the other players.

2. The players stand 10 paces away and shout, "What's the time, Mr Wolf?".

3. If Mr Wolf shouts, "It's 10 o'clock", the players take 10 steps towards Mr Wolf.

4. Watch out because when Mr Wolf shouts "Dinnertime", he chases the other players and whoever he catches is out of the game!

▼ When African hunting dogs pursue their prey, such as the wildebeest, the chase may go on for several kilometres, but the dogs rarely give up. They wait until their prey tires, then leap in for the kill.

22 African wild dogs are deadly pack hunters. They work as a team to chase and torment their prey. The whole pack shares the meal, tearing at the meat with their sharp teeth.

Ambush and attack

23 Lurking beneath the surface of the water, a deadly hunter waits, ready to pounce. Lying absolutely still, only its eyes and nostrils are visible. With one swift movement, the victim is dragged underwater. This killer is the crocodile, a relative of the dinosaurs.

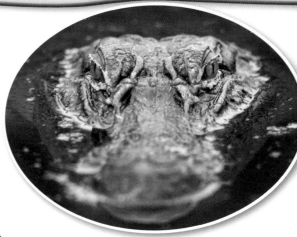

▲ Crocodiles and alligators are well-suited to their aquatic lifestyle. They spend much of their day in water, keeping cool and hidden from view.

24 When a crocodile has its prey in sight, it moves at lightning speed. The prey has little chance to escape as the crocodile pulls it underwater. Gripping the victim in its mighty jaws, the crocodile twists and turns in a 'deathspin' until its victim has drowned.

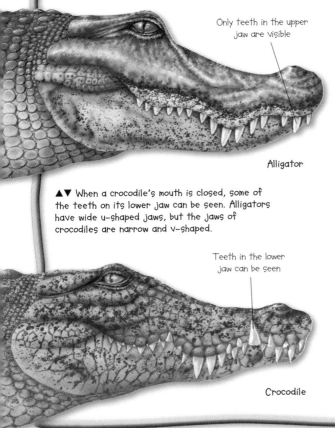

Only teeth in the upper jaw are visible

Alligator

▲▼ When a crocodile's mouth is closed, some of the teeth on its lower jaw can be seen. Alligators have wide u-shaped jaws, but the jaws of crocodiles are narrow and v-shaped.

Teeth in the lower jaw can be seen

Crocodile

25 The largest crocodiles in the world live in estuaries, where rivers meet the oceans. They are called estuarine crocodiles and can reach a staggering 7 metres in length. These giant predators are often known as man-eating crocodiles, although they are most likely to catch turtles, snakes, monkeys, cows and pigs.

26 Alligators are very strong reptiles with wide jaws and thick, scaly skin on their backs. They live in marshes, ponds and rivers, often close to where people live. Like all crocodiles and alligators, the American alligator will catch and eat anything. They have even been known to attack humans.

▼ Crocodiles and alligators have huge jaws, full of teeth. As well as being used for grabbing and holding prey, they use their teeth to slice pieces from the body of the victim.

Mighty monsters

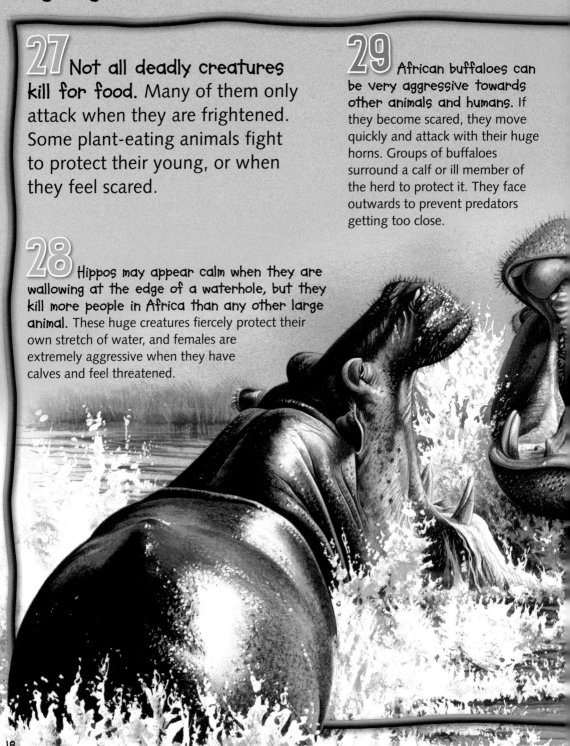

27 Not all deadly creatures kill for food. Many of them only attack when they are frightened. Some plant-eating animals fight to protect their young, or when they feel scared.

28 Hippos may appear calm when they are wallowing at the edge of a waterhole, but they kill more people in Africa than any other large animal. These huge creatures fiercely protect their own stretch of water, and females are extremely aggressive when they have calves and feel threatened.

29 African buffaloes can be very aggressive towards other animals and humans. If they become scared, they move quickly and attack with their huge horns. Groups of buffaloes surround a calf or ill member of the herd to protect it. They face outwards to prevent predators getting too close.

30 If an elephant starts flapping its ears and trumpeting, it is giving a warning sign to stay away. However, when an elephant folds its ears back, curls its trunk under its mouth and begins to run – then it really means business. Elephants will attack to keep other animals or humans away from the infants in their herd, and males will fight one another for a mate.

31 With huge bodies and massive horns, rhinos look like fearsome predators. They are actually related to horses and eat a diet of leaves, grass and fruit. Rhinos can become aggressive, however, when they are scared. They have poor eyesight, which may be why they can easily feel confused or threatened, and attack without warning.

◄ Male hippos fight one another using their massive teeth as weapons. Severe injuries can occur, leading to the death of at least one of the hippos.

I DON'T BELIEVE IT!

Adult male elephants are called bulls, and they can become killers. A single stab from an elephant's tusk is enough to cause a fatal wound, and one elephant is strong enough to flip a car over onto its side!

Dragons and monsters

▼ Komodo dragons use their powerful jaws to tear the flesh of their victim, and then eat everything, including bones and fur.

32 **Komodo dragons are not really dragons, but lizards.** They can reach 3 metres in length and up to 100 kilograms in weight, making them the largest lizards in the world. They hunt their prey using their sensitive sense of smell.

33 **Komodos are venomous!** Their sharp teeth tear into their victim's flesh, making wounds into which venom seeps from glands in their jaws. Even if the injured animal escapes the Komodo's clutches, it will probably die from the effects of the venom.

QUIZ

1. What colour is the Gila monster?

2. Why does the fire salamander have bold patterns on its skin?

3. How does the Komodo dragon hunt its prey?

Answers:
1. Black, pink and yellow
2. To warn predators that it is poisonous 3. Using its sensitive sense of smell

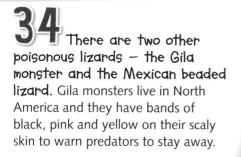

34 There are two other poisonous lizards — the Gila monster and the Mexican beaded lizard. Gila monsters live in North America and they have bands of black, pink and yellow on their scaly skin to warn predators to stay away.

▲ Gila monsters use their sense of smell to hunt small animals and find reptile eggs. They can kill their prey with a single bite.

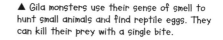

▼ Fire salamanders are amphibians, like frogs. They hunt insects and earthworms, mainly at night.

35 Fire salamanders look like a cross between a lizard and a frog. They have bold patterns on their skin to warn predators that they are poisonous. The poison, or toxin, is on their skin and tastes foul. They squirt the toxin at predators, irritating or even killing them.

Fearsome frogs

36 **At first glance, few frogs appear fearsome.** They may not have teeth or claws, but frogs and toads produce a deadly substance in their moist skin. This substance may taste foul or even be poisonous. The most poisonous frogs live in the forests of Central and South America. They are called poison-dart frogs.

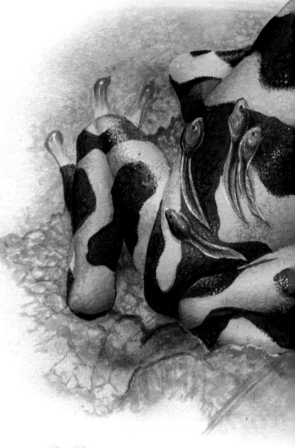

37 **One of the deadliest frogs is the golden poison-dart frog.** It lives in rainforests in western Colombia, and its skin produces a very powerful poison – one of the deadliest known substances. A single touch is enough to cause almost instant death.

▼ The strawberry poison-dart frog is also known as the 'blue jeans' frog because of its blue legs.

38 **Many poison-dart frogs are becoming rare in the wild.** This is because the rainforests where they live are being cut down. Some poison-dart frogs can be kept in captivity, where they gradually become less poisonous. When they are raised in captivity, these frogs are not poisonous at all.

◄ The male green poison-dart frog carries tadpoles on his back. He takes them to a safe place in water where they will grow into adults.

I DON'T BELIEVE IT!

Poison-dart frogs are brightly coloured or boldly patterned. Their jewel-like appearance warns predators to stay away. This means that these frogs can hunt for bugs during the day, without fear of being eaten.

40 People who live in the rainforests of Central and South America use the poison from frogs to catch food. A hunter wipes the tip of a dart on the poisonous frog's back, then carefully puts it in a blowpipe. One puff sends the lethal dart into the body of an unsuspecting monkey or bird.

▼ Poison is wiped off the back of the golden poison-dart frog with a dart. One frog produces enough poison for more than 50 darts.

39 Looking after eggs is the job of male green poison-dart frogs. The female lays her eggs amongst the leaf litter on the forest floor. The male guards them until they hatch into tadpoles, then carries them to water, where they will grow into frogs.

Eight-legged hunters

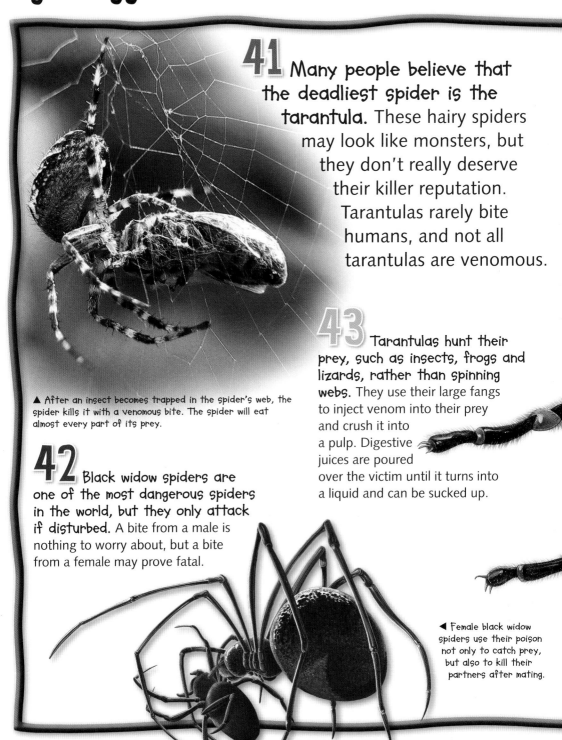

41 Many people believe that the deadliest spider is the tarantula. These hairy spiders may look like monsters, but they don't really deserve their killer reputation. Tarantulas rarely bite humans, and not all tarantulas are venomous.

▲ After an insect becomes trapped in the spider's web, the spider kills it with a venomous bite. The spider will eat almost every part of its prey.

42 Black widow spiders are one of the most dangerous spiders in the world, but they only attack if disturbed. A bite from a male is nothing to worry about, but a bite from a female may prove fatal.

43 Tarantulas hunt their prey, such as insects, frogs and lizards, rather than spinning webs. They use their large fangs to inject venom into their prey and crush it into a pulp. Digestive juices are poured over the victim until it turns into a liquid and can be sucked up.

◄ Female black widow spiders use their poison not only to catch prey, but also to kill their partners after mating.

44 Spiders belong to a group of animals called arachnids, along with scorpions and ticks. Some ticks can kill without using deadly poison. They attach themselves to the bodies of humans and other animals, and suck their blood. This can spread deadly diseases.

QUIZ

1. How do ticks kill animals?
2. Is the male or female black widow spider more dangerous?
3. Which spider stands on its hind legs when it feels threatened?

Answers:
1. They suck their blood and spread diseases
2. Female 3. Funnel web spider

45 There are many types of funnel web spider, and some of them are very venomous. When a funnel web spider is threatened, it stands on its hind legs and rears, showing its huge fangs. These killers bite their prey many times, injecting poison.

▲ The fangs of the funnel web spider are so strong that they can pierce human skin, even fingernails. Its bite can cause death in just 15 minutes.

Clever defenders

46 To survive in a dangerous world, animals need to be able to hide, fight, or appear deadly. When it is threatened, the spiny puffer fish swallows large amounts of water, making its body swell up and its spines stand on end.

47 Spines can be used to pass venom into the victim's body, or used as weapons of defence. The long, sharp spines on the Cape porcupine are called quills, and they stick into an attacker's body, causing painful injuries.

▼▶ The spiny puffer fish stiffens and swells its body, changing from an ordinary-looking fish to a spiky ball.

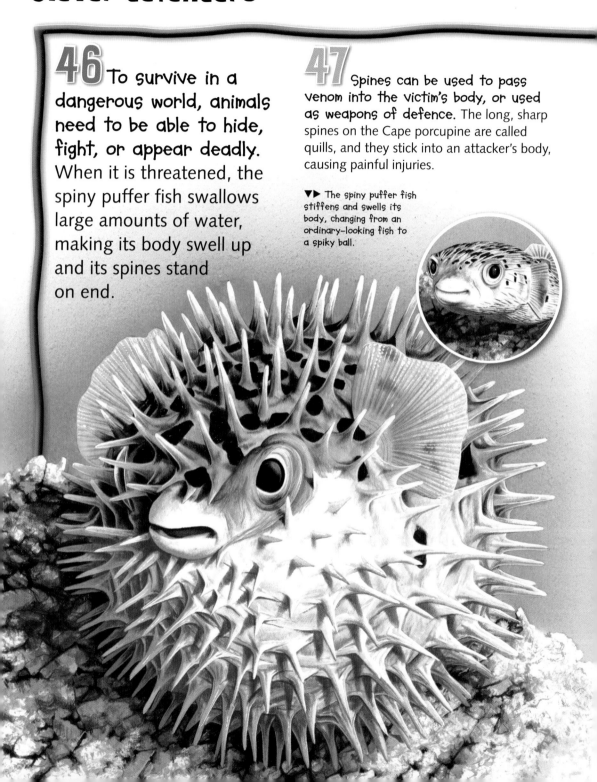

◀ Tortoises are protected from predators by their tough shell. Even the sharp claws and teeth of lion cubs cannot break it.

48
Some animals hide from their predators using camouflage. This means the colour or pattern of an animal's skin blends in with its surroundings. Lizards called chameleons are masters of camouflage. They can change their skin colour from brown to green so they blend in with their background. They do this to communicate with one another.

49
The bold colours and pattern on the coral snake's skin warns predators that it is poisonous. The milk snake looks almost identical to the coral snake, but it is not venomous. Its colour keeps it safe though, because predators think it is poisonous.

I DON'T BELIEVE IT!
Electric eels have an unusual way of staying safe – they zap prey and predators with electricity! They can produce 600 volts of power at a time, which is enough to kill a human!

▶ The harmless milk snake looks similar to the venomous coral snake, so predators stay away. This life-saving animal trick is called mimicry.

27

Danger at sea

50 Deep in the ocean lurk some of the deadliest creatures in the world. There are keen-eyed killers, venomous stingers and sharp-toothed hunters, but as few of these animals come into contact with humans, attacks are rare.

▶ The Australian box jellyfish is also known as the sea wasp. Its tentacles can grow more than 3 metres in length and one animal has enough venom to kill 60 people.

51 Barracudas are long, strong, powerful fish. They lunge at their prey, baring dagger-like teeth. Although they prey on other fish, barracudas may mistake swimmers for food and attack them.

52 The box jellyfish is one of the most lethal creatures in the world. A touch from only one tentacle can kill a human. The floating body of a jellyfish is harmless, but danger lies in the many tentacles that drift below. Each tentacle is covered with tiny stingers that shoot venom into the victim.

◀ Barracudas are fierce fish with powerful jaws and sharp teeth.

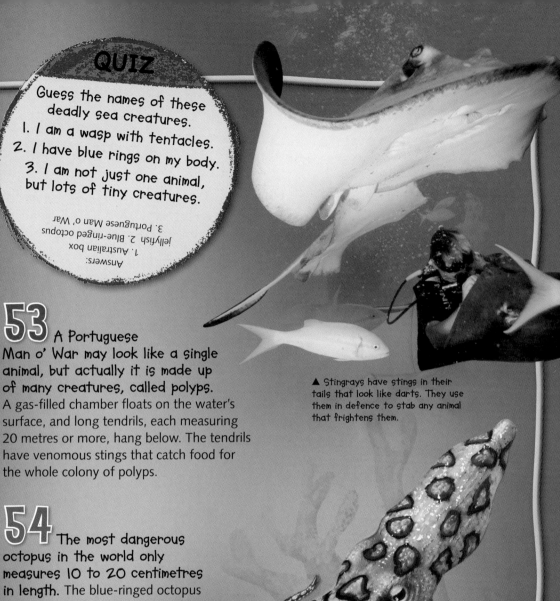

53 A Portuguese Man o' War may look like a single animal, but actually it is made up of many creatures, called polyps. A gas-filled chamber floats on the water's surface, and long tendrils, each measuring 20 metres or more, hang below. The tendrils have venomous stings that catch food for the whole colony of polyps.

▲ Stingrays have stings in their tails that look like darts. They use them in defence to stab any animal that frightens them.

54 The most dangerous octopus in the world only measures 10 to 20 centimetres in length. The blue-ringed octopus grabs prey with its tentacles and then bites deeply, injecting venom into the victim. The venom can kill a human in just four minutes.

▶ The tiny blue-ringed octopus has enough venom to kill ten people.

Sharks in the shadows

55 Few animals send a shiver down the spine quite like a great white shark. This huge fish is a skilled hunter. Its bullet-shaped body can slice through the water at lightning speed, powered by huge muscles and a crescent-shaped tail.

56 Sharks are fish, and belong to the same family as rays and skates. Most sharks are predators and feed on fish, squid, seals and other sea creatures. Some sharks hunt with quick spurts of energy as they chase their prey. Others lie in wait for victims to pass by.

57 One of the deadliest sharks can be found in oceans and seas throughout the world. Blue sharks often hunt in packs and circle their prey before attacking. Although these creatures normally eat fish and squid, they will attack humans.

58 Bull sharks are a deadly threat to humans. This is because they live in areas close to human homes. They often swim inland, using the same rivers that people use to bathe and collect water, and may attack.

▲ Great white sharks are fearsome predators. They have rows of ultra-sharp triangular teeth that are perfect for taking large bites out of prey, such as seals, sea lions and dolphins.

59 Grey reef sharks are sleek, swift predators of the Indian and Pacific oceans. Unusually, they give plenty of warning before they attack. If the grey reef shark feels threatened, it drops its fins down, raises its snout and starts weaving and rolling through the water.

Peril at the shore

▼ When the stonefish's spines are touched, venom is released from the gland at the base. The venom can cause breathing difficulties and heart failure.

Sharp tip

Venom canal

Venom gland

▲ While hidden amongst rocks, the camouflaged stonefish waits for its prey, such as small fish.

60 The seashore may seem like a quiet place, but danger lies beneath the gently lapping waves. While some predators actively hunt their prey, some creatures just sit and wait.

61 Stonefish may look like a piece of rocky coral, but their cunning disguise hides a deadly surprise. One touch of the sharp spines on the stonefish's back results in an injection of venom, which may be fatal.

63 **Sea snakes spend their lives in water.** They breathe air, so they need to keep returning to the surface. All sea snakes are poisonous, and although their bites are painless at first, the venom is very powerful and can kill.

64 **Seashells are not always as harmless as they appear.** Rather than chasing their prey, cone shells attack other animals using a poison that paralyzes the victim so it cannot escape. The venom of fish-eating cone shells can paralyze a fish within seconds. Although their venom can be fatal to humans, it is being used by scientists to develop medicines that reduce pain.

62 **Lionfish are graceful swimmers, but the long spines on their fins inject venom as swiftly as a needle.** A single injury from one spine causes immediate sickness and great pain, but it is unlikely to prove deadly to a human.

▼ Cone shells use their long proboscis to shoot a poisonous dart into their prey. The venom is very powerful and quickly paralyzes the prey.

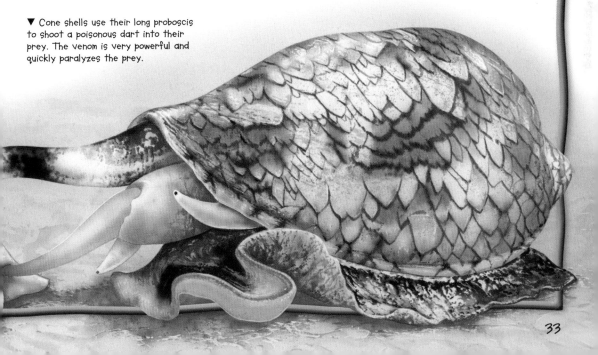

Minibeasts

◀ Although houseflies do not have stings, they are dangerous to humans. They can spread diseases if they land on food.

65 **Animals don't have to be big to be beastly.** There are many small animals, particularly insects, that are killers. Some of them, such as ants, are predators that hunt to eat. Others, such as locusts, cause destruction that affects humans.

66 **Ants are found almost everywhere, except in water.** Most ants are harmless to humans, but army ants and driver ants turn tropical forests and woodlands into battlefields. The stings of army ants contain chemicals that dissolve flesh. Once their prey has turned to liquid, the ants can begin to drink it.

▼ Millions of army ants live in a single group, or colony. They hunt together, swarming through leaf litter and attacking anything in their way.

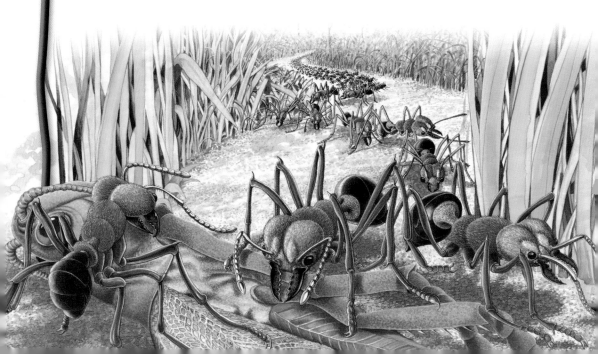

67 Driver ants have large jaws that can slice easily through food. They hunt in large numbers and swarm through forests hunting for prey. Driver ants can kill large animals, such as cows, by biting them to death. They have also been known to strip a chicken down to its skeleton in less than a day.

68 Deadly plagues of locusts have been written about for thousands of years. When they search for food, they travel in swarms of millions, eating all the plants they encounter. This can leave humans without any food.

▲ Killer bees fiercely protect their hive by swarming around it. They will attack anything that approaches the nest.

69 Killer bees are a new type of bee that was created by a scientist. He was hoping to breed bees that made lots of honey, but the bees proved to be extremely aggressive. Killer bees swarm in huge groups and when one bee stings, the others quickly join in. One sting is not deadly, but lots of bee stings can kill a human. It is thought that about 1000 people have been killed by these minibeasts.

The enemy within

70 Many deadly creatures are too small to be seen. They are parasites, living on or inside the body of humans or animals, causing harm, disease and even death. An animal that is home to a parasite is called a host.

▼ The Black Death, or bubonic plague, was spread by rats and it wiped out one-third of Europe's population (25 million people) about 700 years ago.

71 Rats are known to spread disease. They carry bacteria on their paws and in their mouths, but they also carry another type of parasite called fleas. Even the fleas can have parasites inside their bodies – plague bacteria.

72 Humans have suffered from plagues for thousands of years. These diseases are spread when rat fleas bite people, spreading the plague bacteria. Plague usually only occurs when people live in dirty conditions where rats and their fleas can breed. Plague can spread quickly, wiping out millions of lives.

▼ Tsetse flies feed on blood and spread parasites that cause sleeping sickness. This painful disease is common in developing countries and leads to death if not treated.

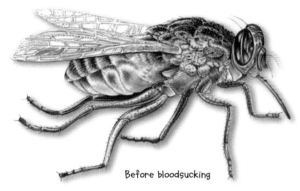

Before bloodsucking

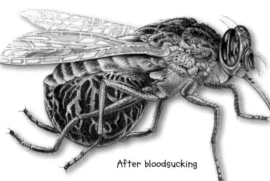

After bloodsucking

74 The mosquito and its tiny parasites are among the deadliest creatures in the world. When mosquitoes suck human and animal blood, they pass parasites into the host's body, including the parasite that causes malaria. Malaria is a disease that mainly affects people living in hot countries in the developing world. It causes about one million deaths a year in Africa.

73 Some of the most common parasites are worms. Tiny threadlike worms called nematodes live inside the bodies of most animals, including some humans. Nematodes can spread disease. Tapeworms belong to a different family of worms called flatworms. They absorb food from their host's intestine.

▶ Mosquitoes pierce the skin of the victim to suck their blood, spreading deadly diseases, such as malaria.

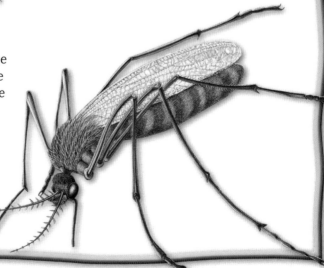

VENOM

75 Venom is the name given to toxic substances made by an animal's body, which can be injected into another creature (or person). A huge variety of animals have developed the use of deadly body chemicals – from tiny spiders to large lizards. The more we know about these incredible creatures and their lethal venoms, the more likely we are able to avoid harm and even save lives.

▶ Spiders inject their venom using sharp fangs. The Sydney funnel–web of Australia has one of the most toxic venoms to humans.

Why have venom?

76 Some hunting animals (called predators) use their sharp teeth and claws to hunt, but venomous animals use deadly chemicals. A venomous predator can inject its victim (the prey), then move to a safe distance and wait for the venom to take effect, avoiding a fight.

77 Some animals can deliver their venom from a distance as well as at close range. Bombardier beetles defend themselves by spraying enemies with a toxic fluid. Some ants can deliver venom in four different ways – bite, tail-sting, or spray from the mouth or rear end.

① Toxin producing gland
② One of two storage reservoirs
③ Enzyme producing gland
④ Explosive chamber

78 The size of a venomous animal is not always linked to its deadliness. Small spiders, such as black widows, have very powerful venom, while big spiders, such as tarantulas, have weaker venom. They make up for it with greater size and strength.

◀ The venom of the cobalt blue tarantula paralyzes its grasshopper prey.

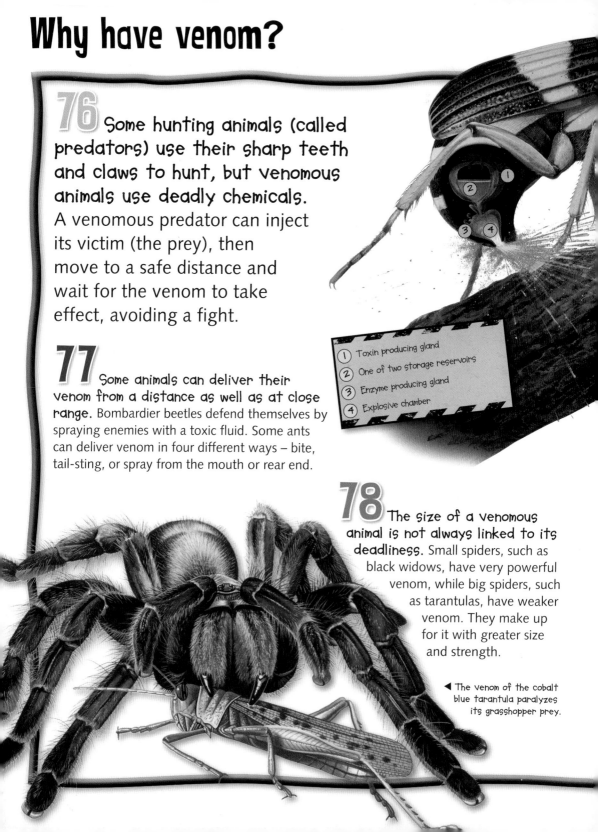

◀ The bombardier beetle mixes two fluids, enzyme and venom, in its rear end. The explosive chemical reaction makes a nasty boiling spray used to protect against attackers, such as army ants.

79 Venom can be used to protect against enemies in self-defence. Fish such as the lesser weeverfish, lizards like the gila monster, and insects such as wasps and bees strike out to protect against predators – they rarely use their venom to hunt. These animals often warn others of their deadliness by displaying bright, bold colours or patterns.

80 Venomous animals don't deliberately seek out humans to bite or sting. An attack usually happens in self-defence because the animal is surprised or feels threatened. Like most wild animals, venomous creatures prefer to avoid attacking large enemies.

▼ Weeverfish live near the sandy sea floor, and often lie mostly buried with just their eyes, mouth and defensive fin spines showing.

Black dorsal fin is connected to venom glands

Venom or poison?

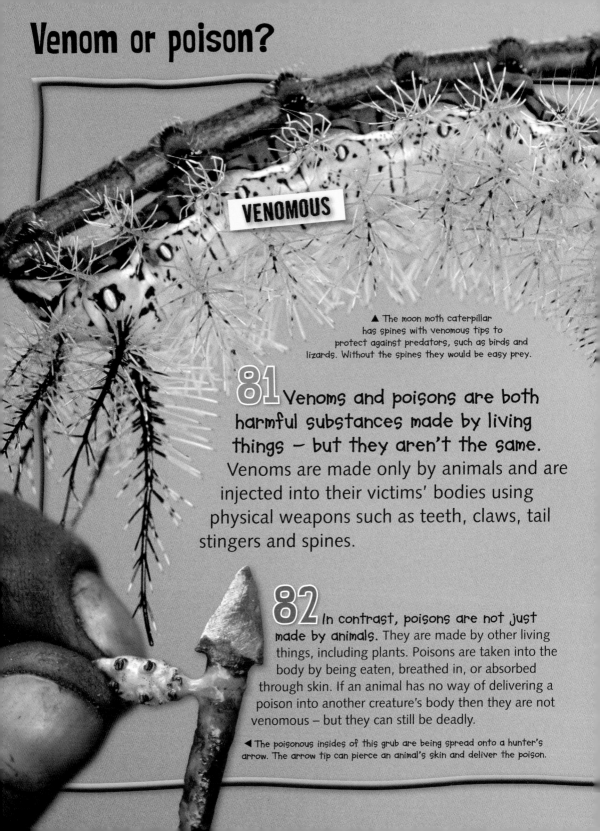

VENOMOUS

▲ The moon moth caterpillar has spines with venomous tips to protect against predators, such as birds and lizards. Without the spines they would be easy prey.

81 Venoms and poisons are both harmful substances made by living things — but they aren't the same. Venoms are made only by animals and are injected into their victims' bodies using physical weapons such as teeth, claws, tail stingers and spines.

82 In contrast, poisons are not just made by animals. They are made by other living things, including plants. Poisons are taken into the body by being eaten, breathed in, or absorbed through skin. If an animal has no way of delivering a poison into another creature's body then they are not venomous — but they can still be deadly.

◀ The poisonous insides of this grub are being spread onto a hunter's arrow. The arrow tip can pierce an animal's skin and deliver the poison.

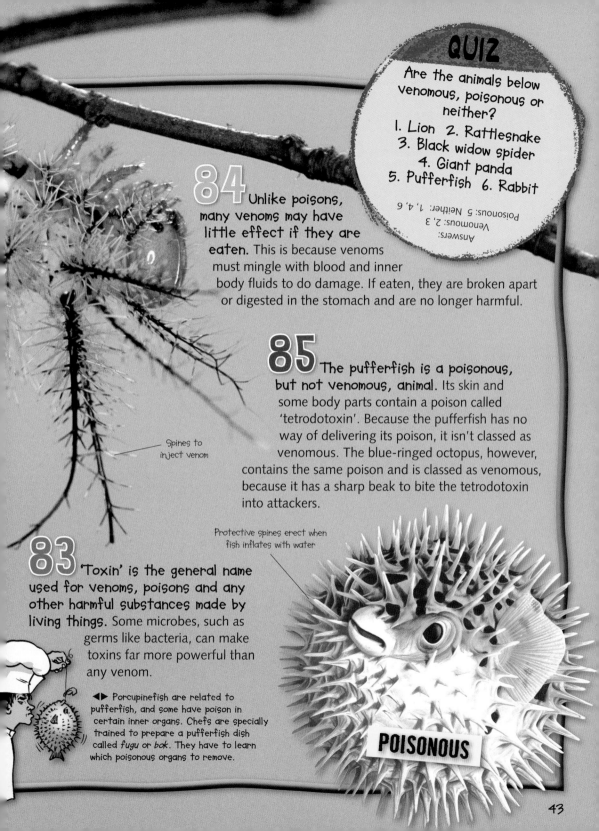

QUIZ

Are the animals below venomous, poisonous or neither?
1. Lion 2. Rattlesnake
3. Black widow spider
4. Giant panda
5. Pufferfish 6. Rabbit

Answers:
Venomous: 2, 3
Poisonous: 5 Neither: 1, 4, 6

84 Unlike poisons, many venoms may have little effect if they are eaten. This is because venoms must mingle with blood and inner body fluids to do damage. If eaten, they are broken apart or digested in the stomach and are no longer harmful.

85 The pufferfish is a poisonous, but not venomous, animal. Its skin and some body parts contain a poison called 'tetrodotoxin'. Because the pufferfish has no way of delivering its poison, it isn't classed as venomous. The blue-ringed octopus, however, contains the same poison and is classed as venomous, because it has a sharp beak to bite the tetrodotoxin into attackers.

Spines to inject venom

Protective spines erect when fish inflates with water

83 'Toxin' is the general name used for venoms, poisons and any other harmful substances made by living things. Some microbes, such as germs like bacteria, can make toxins far more powerful than any venom.

◀▶ Porcupinefish are related to pufferfish, and some have poison in certain inner organs. Chefs are specially trained to prepare a pufferfish dish called *fugu* or *bok*. They have to learn which poisonous organs to remove.

POISONOUS

43

Potent poisons

BEWARE! POISONOUS

▶ Monkshood poison can pass through the skin.

86 Lots of living things use poisons for self-defence. Plants use poisons to deter animals from eating them. In some plants, such as deadly nightshade, almost every part is poisonous. In others, only certain parts such as the leaves are poisonous.

▲ Fly agaric toadstools can make people sick, dizzy and even collapse if eaten.

▲ The harmless-looking death cap mushroom kills many people each year.

87 Many animals use poison for protection, too. Marine toads are the largest toads in the world, and when threatened they produce a poisonous substance from glands in their skin. The toxin is not used to kill prey, but to protect the toad from being eaten by other animals.

▶ The marine toad's foul-tasting poison is produced in glands behind its eyes and on its back. It causes sickness, numbness and hallucinations if taken into the body.

Poison seeps from glands

Poisonous
skin

▲ The strawberry poison-dart frog's bright colours
advertise its poisonous skin to possible attackers.

90 Some fish have horrible-tasting, poisonous flesh and skin. They include the pufferfish, cowfish, oilfish and jack. They are mostly slow-swimming fish – they have no need to race away and escape from predators, who avoid them.

88 Frogs, toads and salamanders are well known for the poisons that ooze from their skin. Small, colourful poison-dart frogs are the most dangerous – one type has poison that could kill dozens of people. Rainforest hunters wipe their arrows and blowpipe darts on its skin to poison the animals they shoot when hunting.

I DON'T BELIEVE IT!
Local people call pitohui birds 'rubbish birds' because they can't be eaten and they have a disgusting smell.

89 Very few birds or mammals are poisonous. Among the few are pitohui birds from Southeast Asia, which have skin and feathers that can cause numbness and tingling when touched, and sickness if people eat them.

▶ The blue-capped ifrita, a relative of pitohui birds, has a similar poison called 'batrachotoxin' in its feathers and skin.

Warning displays

91 Some venomous and poisonous animals display colours, sounds and other features. This is known as 'aposematism'. It allows other creatures to recognize them as potentially dangerous and avoid them. Young predators may try to attack venomous animals at first, but will soon learn from painful experience to stay away.

▲ Yellow and black are common warning colours, shown here on a fire salamander, which has poisonous skin.

▼ The lionfish's colourful, elaborate fins show that its dorsal (back) fin spines can jab in very powerful venom.

92 Bright colours and patterns are common signs that warn of venom or poison. Common examples are black with yellow or orange, as in wasps, bees, salamanders and gila monster lizards. Red and black occur in venomous redback spiders and horrible-tasting ladybirds.

Venomous
dorsal spines

SQUEAK!

93 Warning sounds include hisses and rattles. Various kinds of insects, toads and snakes hiss to tell enemies that they are poisonous or venomous. The rattlesnake's rattling tail is another warning sound. It means that the snake is alert and ready to strike, or bite, to defend itself.

▶ Velvet 'ants' are actually wasps. They chirp or squeak as a warning before delivering their painful sting.

Cobra hood spread wide

94 Certain types of movements and body postures also act as warnings. If a cobra spreads out the hood of skin on either side of its neck, it means: 'I'm ready to bite and stab in my venom!' Skunks hop about and even do handstands to warn that they are ready to spray their foul-smelling, horrible-tasting fluid!

Mongoose about to attack

▲ Cobras rear up and spread their neck hood when preparing to strike at predators such as a mongoose.

95 These methods of self-defence help avoid a real battle. By fighting they risk getting injured or using up all of their venom. Avoiding a battle is much better than having one.

CREATE A KILLER CREATURE

You will need:
paper   coloured pens or pencils
Draw a venomous animal using different body parts from creatures in this book. It could have a snake's head, a wasp's body and a scorpion's tail.

Venomous to who?

I DON'T BELIEVE IT!

Long ago some people believed a venomous bite from a spider or snake would help to purify the body and drive away evil spirits – provided it did not kill you!

96 Many animals are venomous – but not to all other creatures, all of the time. Whether a creature can use its venom effectively depends on many things – especially on what kind of animal it chooses to bite or sting.

97 What people often mean by the term 'venomous' is whether the venom affects humans. For an animal to be considered venomous it needs to be able to puncture human skin. If it can, the venom needs to be powerful enough to do harm. If the animal can't achieve these things, it isn't venomous to us.

▼ The black widow spider is small but has sharp fangs stong enough to pierce human skin.

▲ The world's fastest snake, the black mamba, has venom so strong it can kill a human in 20 minutes.

98 How venomous an animal is depends on its health and strength. Also, if the animal strikes hard it is more dangerous than if it just gives a quick warning bite – some snakes will give attackers a quick jab, alerting them to their deadliness, but save the full impact of their venom for their prey.

99 Many people are terrified of house spiders.
But small-to-medium ones can't pierce human skin. Really large house spiders can just about make a puncture, but they rarely do unless severely provoked. Still, their bite is rarely serious.

▶ The cellar spider looks slim and weak, but it catches and eats big house spiders. In humans its bite causes a burning feeling.

▶ There are several ways to measure venom strength.

100 Humans are quite big compared to most venomous animals and so often need to be injected with lots of venom to cause real harm.
A small caterpillar or fly, with thin skin, needs much less venom. The red-banded digger wasp has venom that easily paralyzes its caterpillar prey but the poison has no paralyzing effect on the human body.

TOXICITY RATING

☠ CHEMICAL TESTS These give the level or concentration of a harmful substance in a venom, such as calciseptine in black mamba venom, which attacks nerves.

☠ BIOLOGICAL TESTS Different amounts of venom are added to microscopic cells in glass tubes or flasks, to see how many cells are damaged or killed.

☠ SPECTROMETRY A venom is put through a machine called a mass spectrometer that shows which harmful substances it contains and how much of each.

▼ This red-banded sand wasp can easily pierce its prey's thin skin to inject paralyzing poison, but human skin is too tough.

Types of venom

101 Venoms are made in body parts called venom glands – but not all venoms are the same. Venomous animals contain various kinds of chemicals that affect different parts of their victims. Some animals can have several types of chemical in their venom.

Wasp

Sting

102 Many of the chemicals in venoms are substances called 'enzymes'. They alter the way living body tissues work. Each body part has thousands of life processes going on inside, which are controlled by enzymes. Venom contains different types of enzymes that interfere, causing the tissues to break apart.

103 Venom chemicals called 'neurotoxins' attack the nervous system. The nervous system is your body's control and communication system, made up of nerves and the brain. Venoms that attack it cause pain, paralysis, numbness and tingling. Neurotoxins can also affect breathing and heartbeat.

Swollen hand due to wasp sting

◀ Wasp sting venom has several toxins that disrupt blood flow, cause swelling and fluid to collect and produce severe pain.

VARIETY OF VENOMS

Type of venom	Effect on the body	Example animal
Myotoxin (proteolytic)	Leads to the break-down of muscle tissue	Sea snake
Cardiotoxin	Causes cardiac arrest (heart failure)	Box jellyfish
Necrotoxin	The main effect is necrosis – the death of body tissues	Brown recluse spider
Haematoxin	Damages blood vessels and causes internal bleeding	Rattlesnakes
Neurotoxin	Severe damage to the nervous system	Blue-ringed octopus

104 Venom chemicals called 'haemotoxins' affect the blood and its circulation (flow) through blood vessels. They cause swelling and bleeding, and the blood may go sticky or clot, so it cannot flow to organs such as the brain. Because blood carries vital oxygen, clots can lead to shortness of breath and even suffocation.

105 Venom chemicals such as necrotoxins and proteolytic enzymes break apart body tissues into a mushy mess. Muscles go soggy and floppy, and skin turns into a goo. The lancehead snake has especially strong proteolytic enzymes.

I DON'T BELIEVE IT!

If certain kinds of strong-biting spiders were the same size as you, their sharp, deadly fangs would be bigger than bananas!

▶ Rattlesnakes have some of the most corrosive venom.

Delivering doses

106 Venomous animals have a wide range of weapons and body parts to deliver venom into their victims. Some animals such as the woolly bear caterpillars, starfish, sea urchins and fish use hairs or spines to break or puncture the skin.

HAIRS

▲ Thin, spiny hairs of woolly-bear caterpillars look soft but easily jab in venom.

107 Some venomous animals such as bees, wasps and scorpions have stingers at their tail end. The scorpion can use its fierce pincers and tail sting together. It raises its pincers and arches its tail over its head, ready to hold its victim and jab venom from above with its sharp tail tip.

▼ The spine tips of crown-of-thorns starfish easily break off, carrying their venom into the skin.

▶ The wasp's venom gland is near the sharp sting at the rear end.

SPINES

STING

Stinger

Sting bulb

Venom gland

Venom sac

FANGS

Venom flows down hollow fangs

◀ The eyelash viper has especially long fangs that jab through the victim's skin into muscles, blood vessels and nerves.

108 **Most venom weapons are located in an animal's head, near the mouth.** Venomous snakes have long teeth (fangs), connected to venom glands behind the eyes. The fangs are often grooved to allow venom to flow into a wound. Spiders also have sharp fangs to pierce their prey and centipedes have venomous front claws to deliver their poison.

▼ In some cases, venom pumps can be applied to bites and stings to remove toxic venom that hasn't gone too deep.

109 **If a person is bitten or stung by a venomous creature it's vital to get expert help fast, even if it does not hurt at first.** The quickest way is usually by calling emergency paramedics or doctors. Meanwhile the person should keep the bitten part lower than the rest of the body, and also stay still, so the venom does not spread around their body.

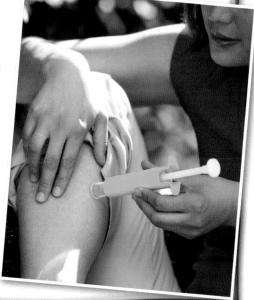

110 **If possible, the venomous animal should be identified, or described carefully to the medical experts.** Then they will know the best treatments to give, such as fast-acting medicines, and an anti-venom to work against that particular venom's effects.

Jelly killers

111 Jellyfish don't look dangerous, but they can be deadly predators. They use stingers called cnidocytes (say 'nido-sites') to deliver venom. Jellyfish belong to the same animal group as sea anemones and coral creatures called polyps.

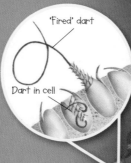

▶ Cnidocytes keep their venom darts coiled up until touched, then fire them out to jab passing victims.

'Fired' dart

Dart in cell

112 Cnidocytes are tiny harpoon–like darts that can only be seen under a microscope. There are hundreds or thousands of them on the tentacles of a jellyfish, anemone or coral polyp. When these micro-stingers rub against something they 'fire' by flicking out their sharp points to jab in venom. Clever boxer crabs have utilized the stinging power of anemones by grasping them in their claws and jabbing would-be predators.

▲ The Portuguese Man o' War's stinging tentacles dangle below the float and main body. They trail for up to 20 metres through the water.

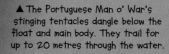

113 Jellyfish, anemones and coral polyps use stingers to paralyze their prey. The tentacles grasp their helpless victim, such as a fish, a shrimp or a worm, then slowly pull it into the mouth.

QUIZ
Which of the animals listed below would a jellyfish catch and eat?
1. Baby fish 2. Blue whales
3. Woodlice 4. Sea-slugs
5. Shrimp 6. Earthworms

Answers:
1, 4 and 5

▼ In the movie *Finding Nemo* (2003), Dory the blue tang fish takes a while to realize that jellyfish can sting.

114 Some of the most venomous marine animals are found in the seas near Australia. The box jellyfish has extremely potent venom, as does the deadly Irukandji jellyfish, which despite its tiny size causes terrible burning pains, sweating, sickness and feelings of panic if stung.

▶ The Irukandji jellyfish's body is only the size of a small grape. The length of the tentacles can vary from a few centimetres up to one metre.

115 Fire corals are named after the burning pain caused by their stings. These small polyp-like creatures build beautiful coral shapes but should be avoided by divers. Sea anemones also have venomous stingers to catch prey, but only a few types are harmful to humans.

◀ ▶ Fire corals form yellow, green and brown branching growths.

Venomous molluscs

116 The mollusc animal group includes snails, slugs, squid and octopus. There are venomous molluscs in the sea that can harm or even kill people. As with most venomous animals, this usually happens by accident – the creature bites or stings in self-defence.

117 A coneshell is a type of sea snail, which jabs a small venom 'harpoon' into its victims. The 'harpoon' is like a little barb or spear made of hard, stony minerals. It is on the end of the coneshell's proboscis, a bendy part like a tiny elephant's trunk. The beautiful colours and patterns of some coneshells attract people, who pick them up only to be stung.

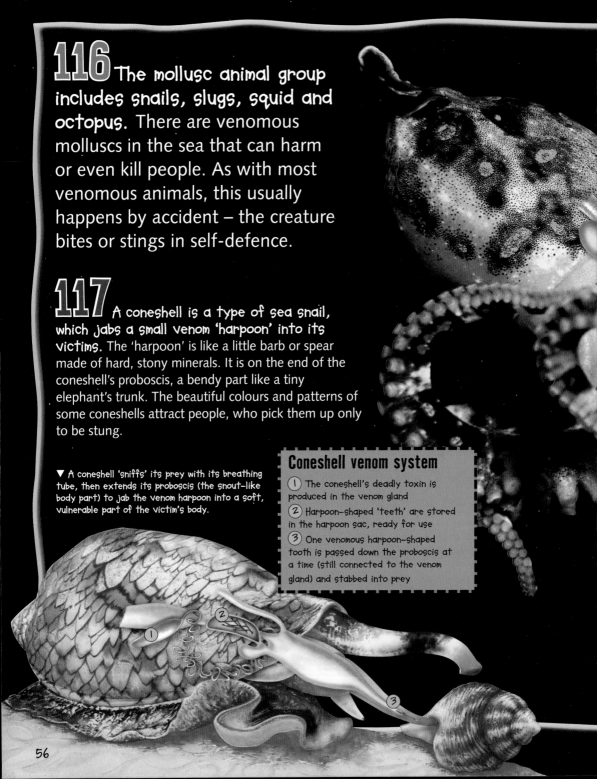

▼ A coneshell 'sniffs' its prey with its breathing tube, then extends its proboscis (the snout–like body part) to jab the venom harpoon into a soft, vulnerable part of the victim's body.

Coneshell venom system

① The coneshell's deadly toxin is produced in the venom gland

② Harpoon–shaped 'teeth' are stored in the harpoon sac, ready for use

③ One venomous harpoon–shaped tooth is passed down the proboscis at a time (still connected to the venom gland) and stabbed into prey

▼ The blue-ringed octopus can spit venom into the water to paralyze its prey or it can bite an enemy to stab in deadly venom.

118 Auger shells are another type of venomous snail. Although not as deadly as coneshells, they too have a harpoon-like barb on a bendy proboscis, which they jab into worms and other victims.

119 The blue-ringed octopus is the most deadly mollusc. Its body is hardly the size of a tennis ball, but its venom is strong enough to kill a human. This small octopus lurks in rock pools. When it feels alarmed and ready to bite, it makes its rings glow bright blue as a warning.

Blue-ringed octopus venom system

① Salivary glands, where the venom is produced and stored

② Sharp, hard beak, used to inject venom

120 Scientists have recently discovered that other kinds of octopus, cuttlefish and squid use venom. These molluscs bite their victims with sharp, beak-like mouthparts to inject venom when attacked. Like the blue-ringed octopus, the venom is in the animals' saliva (spit).

◄ This flamboyant cuttlefish changes colour in a flash to warn other animals of its venomous bite.

Insect slayers

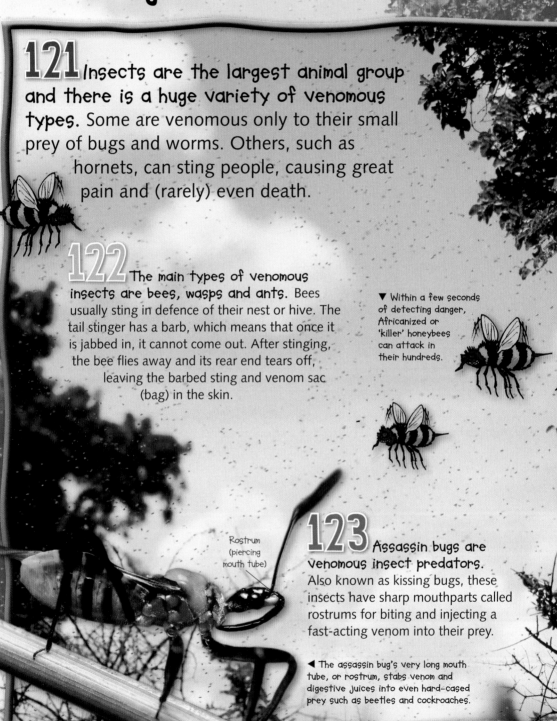

121 Insects are the largest animal group and there is a huge variety of venomous types. Some are venomous only to their small prey of bugs and worms. Others, such as hornets, can sting people, causing great pain and (rarely) even death.

122 The main types of venomous insects are bees, wasps and ants. Bees usually sting in defence of their nest or hive. The tail stinger has a barb, which means that once it is jabbed in, it cannot come out. After stinging, the bee flies away and its rear end tears off, leaving the barbed sting and venom sac (bag) in the skin.

▼ Within a few seconds of detecting danger, Africanized or 'killer' honeybees can attack in their hundreds.

Rostrum (piercing mouth tube)

123 Assassin bugs are venomous insect predators. Also known as kissing bugs, these insects have sharp mouthparts called rostrums for biting and injecting a fast-acting venom into their prey.

◄ The assassin bug's very long mouth tube, or rostrum, stabs venom and digestive juices into even hard-cased prey such as beetles and cockroaches.

124 **Wasps have similar tail stingers to bees, but often the barb is small or missing and their stinger can be used several times.** The wasp's sting is mainly for paralyzing or killing prey such as worms, caterpillars and bugs. It then takes its prey back to its young in their nest. Some even lay their eggs on the paralyzed victim, providing their young with food when they hatch.

▲ The Asian giant hornet has eight toxins in its tail-sting venom. But usually it tackles prey such as bees by cutting off their heads with its powerful mouthparts.

125 **Ants attack their prey in two main ways.** Some have proper stingers, while others bite with their sharp mouths and then spray venom from their rear end into the bite wound. Bullet ants are huge insects and their stings are said to be more painful than any other insect – up to 30 times worse than a wasp sting!

QUIZ
1. What are assassin bugs also known as?
2. Do bullet ants sting or bite venom into prey?
3. Which insect leaves behind a stinger after injecting venom?

Answer:
1. Kissing bugs
2. Sting 3. Bee

▲ Bullet ants grow to 3 centimetres long and sting small creatures such as spiders and bugs to take back to the nest.

Venom duct

Stinger

Dangerous spiders

126 Spiders belong to the arachnid animal group. They have eight legs and nearly all have venom for killing or disabling prey, or for use in self-defence.

127 Most tarantula spiders aren't very venomous, so they use their size and strength to kill prey. The fringed ornamental tarantula is popular as a pet, but its venom can cause great pain, paralysis, sickness and exhaustion.

▼ The Brazilian wandering spider is so-called because it actively searches for prey. When attacking small animals, such as this poison-dart frog, it only needs to inject a tiny drop of its powerful venom.

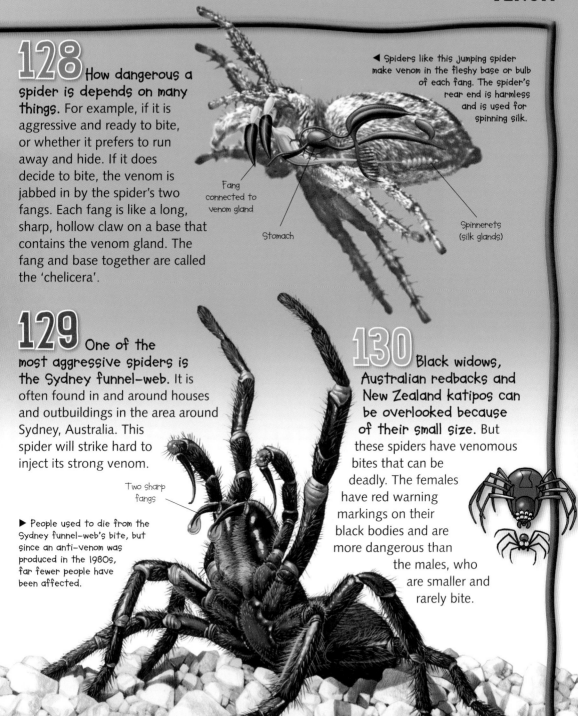

128 How dangerous a spider is depends on many things. For example, if it is aggressive and ready to bite, or whether it prefers to run away and hide. If it does decide to bite, the venom is jabbed in by the spider's two fangs. Each fang is like a long, sharp, hollow claw on a base that contains the venom gland. The fang and base together are called the 'chelicera'.

◄ Spiders like this jumping spider make venom in the fleshy base or bulb of each fang. The spider's rear end is harmless and is used for spinning silk.

Fang connected to venom gland

Stomach

Spinnerets (silk glands)

129 One of the most aggressive spiders is the Sydney funnel-web. It is often found in and around houses and outbuildings in the area around Sydney, Australia. This spider will strike hard to inject its strong venom.

Two sharp fangs

► People used to die from the Sydney funnel-web's bite, but since an anti-venom was produced in the 1980s, far fewer people have been affected.

130 Black widows, Australian redbacks and New Zealand katipos can be overlooked because of their small size. But these spiders have venomous bites that can be deadly. The females have red warning markings on their black bodies and are more dangerous than the males, who are smaller and rarely bite.

Scorpions and centipedes

131 Nearly all kinds of scorpion have a venomous tail stinger. They stab toxins into their prey when hunting or during self-defence. When a scorpion is about to sting, it arches its tail over its back and raises the sharp tip, called the 'telson', above its head.

132 The emperor scorpion is one of the biggest types – it can grow up to 23 centimetres in length. But it is not deadly – its sting feels more like a bee sting. Smaller types, such as the dark-coloured fat-tailed scorpions and the pale death stalker from Africa and the Middle East, are much more dangerous.

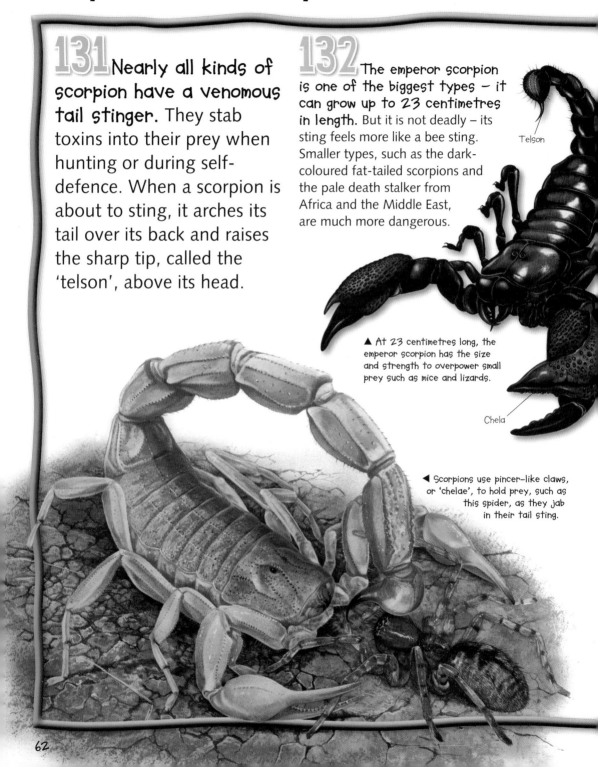

Telson

▲ At 23 centimetres long, the emperor scorpion has the size and strength to overpower small prey such as mice and lizards.

Chela

◀ Scorpions use pincer–like claws, or 'chelae', to hold prey, such as this spider, as they jab in their tail sting.

▲ The giant tropical centipede grows over 30 centimetres in length. Pain from its bite lasts several days.

133 Most scorpions come out at night to hunt small creatures such as bugs, spiders and worms. By day they hide in dark places such as tree holes and under bark and rocks. But they can also wander near humans and hide in boots, drawers, cupboards and under beds.

▲ This centipede's head shows its two feelers or antennae. Below are the two curved, pointed poison claws, almost touching.

134 Centipedes are cousins of spiders and insects, but they have many more legs – and all are venomous. Their first pair of legs is specialized as long, sharp claws called forcipules, which look like pincers under the head. They are designed to stab prey and inject venom.

▶ Most centipedes, like this long–legged centipede, hunt small creatures at night.

135 Giant tropical centipedes such as *Scolopendra gigantea*, can cause great pain to humans. Luckily their bites are hardly ever deadly. Smaller kinds such as the yellow-legged centipede *Parotostigmus* have more powerful venom.

Stars and spines

136 Starfish and sea urchins belong to the 'echinoderm' animal group and are marine animals. There are several venomous kinds but they only use venom for defence – not to catch food.

137 The crown-of-thorns starfish is covered by fierce-looking spines. Each spine has an outer layer or sheath containing venom. If this jabs into human skin it causes great pain and feelings of sickness, which can last for more than a day. These starfish grow to over 50 centimetres across.

▼ Divers in the Indian and Pacific Oceans know never to touch the crown-of-thorns starfish. Its spines can even prick through gloves or wetsuits.

138 Sea urchins have long spines for protection, and also tiny stalked pincers for keeping themselves clean. Both of these can stab venom through human skin, even if touched very gently. The spine tips break easily and may get stuck in the skin, causing pain and swelling that can last for days.

139 Fire urchins have dangerous spines with enlarged tips that contain venom. This produces a stinging, throbbing feeling around the wound where the spines entered the skin. The diadema or needle-spined sea urchin has spine tips so thin you can't see where they end!

140 Sea cucumbers are also echinoderms. They have poisonous body parts called Cuverian organs, which they squirt from their rear end to defend themselves. If these parts touch a wound or sore in the skin, the poison can work like venom and cause numbness, tingling and pain.

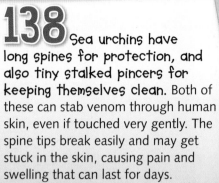

Flower urchins of the Pacific and Indian Oceans have an especially nasty venom delivered by their waving mini-pincers on bendy stalks, called 'pedicellariae'.

Fire urchins are flame-coloured and cause burning pain with their venomous spines, which continually move and wave on their ball-shaped bodies.

The sea cucumber's favourite defence is to squirt out half-digested food, bodily waste, stringy slime, various poisonous body parts—or all of these!

Venomous fish

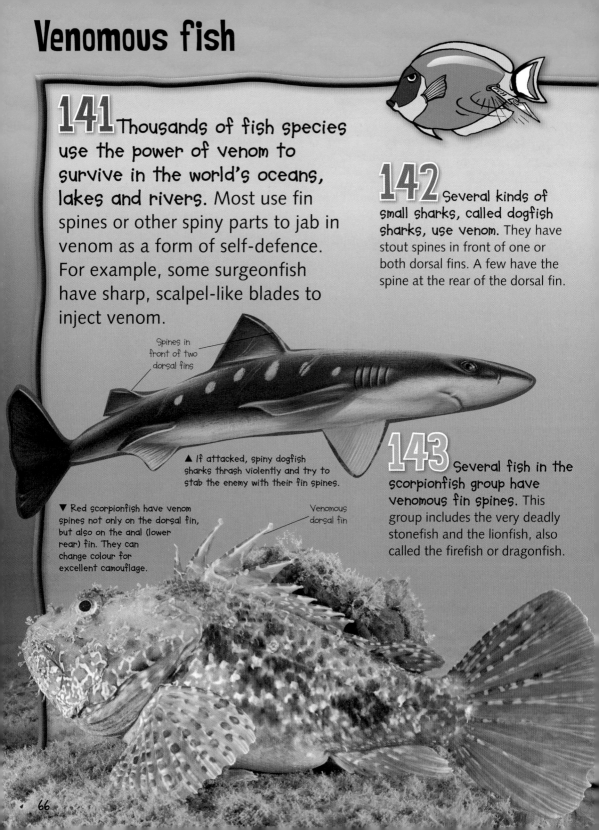

141 Thousands of fish species use the power of venom to survive in the world's oceans, lakes and rivers. Most use fin spines or other spiny parts to jab in venom as a form of self-defence. For example, some surgeonfish have sharp, scalpel-like blades to inject venom.

142 Several kinds of small sharks, called dogfish sharks, use venom. They have stout spines in front of one or both dorsal fins. A few have the spine at the rear of the dorsal fin.

Spines in front of two dorsal fins

▲ If attacked, spiny dogfish sharks thrash violently and try to stab the enemy with their fin spines.

▼ Red scorpionfish have venom spines not only on the dorsal fin, but also on the anal (lower rear) fin. They can change colour for excellent camouflage.

Venomous dorsal fin

143 Several fish in the scorpionfish group have venomous fin spines. This group includes the very deadly stonefish and the lionfish, also called the firefish or dragonfish.

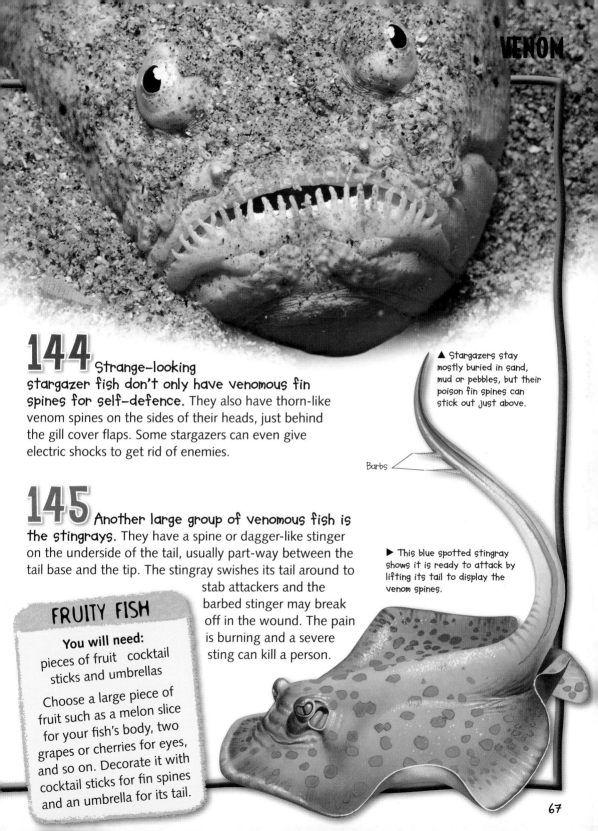

144 Strange-looking stargazer fish don't only have venomous fin spines for self-defence. They also have thorn-like venom spines on the sides of their heads, just behind the gill cover flaps. Some stargazers can even give electric shocks to get rid of enemies.

▲ Stargazers stay mostly buried in sand, mud or pebbles, but their poison fin spines can stick out just above.

Barbs

145 Another large group of venomous fish is the stingrays. They have a spine or dagger-like stinger on the underside of the tail, usually part-way between the tail base and the tip. The stingray swishes its tail around to stab attackers and the barbed stinger may break off in the wound. The pain is burning and a severe sting can kill a person.

▶ This blue spotted stingray shows it is ready to attack by lifting its tail to display the venom spines.

FRUITY FISH

You will need:
pieces of fruit   cocktail sticks and umbrellas

Choose a large piece of fruit such as a melon slice for your fish's body, two grapes or cherries for eyes, and so on. Decorate it with cocktail sticks for fin spines and an umbrella for its tail.

67

Lethal lizards

146 Compared to their reptile cousins, there are far fewer venomous lizards than snakes. Even so, the number could be up to 100 – with more discovered each year. There are only a few lizards with venom strong enough to harm humans.

Venom gland

Sharp, grooved teeth

▲ Gila monsters grow to 60 centimetres in length and are stocky, powerful lizards. They live in dry scrub and desert habitats (homes).

147 Two well known venomous lizards are the gila monster and the beaded lizard, of North and Central America. Like snakes, their venom is a type of saliva. These two lizards produce venom in glands in the lower jaw (unlike snakes, which have glands in the upper jaw).

148 The gila monster and beaded lizard are closely related and use their venom in similar ways. Each lizard bites its prey and chews. The venom oozes along its jaws and teeth into the victim. These lizards can bite very hard for a long time. The venom causes great pain and swelling but it is not deadly to humans.

During defense displays, the lizard extends its 'beard'

If a gila monster lizard bites, it usually hangs on so hard that the only way to loosen its grip is to put the whole lizard underwater.

Sharp spines on the throat

▲ Bearded dragon lizards have tiny glands along both the upper and lower jaws that may produce a weak venom.

149 The Komodo dragon has a venomous bite. For a long time scientists thought that the lizard's victims died quickly from germs seeping into wounds made by its bites. But more recently a substance in its saliva was found to be actually venomous.

150 The Komodo dragon is a type of monitor lizard. Other monitors are also being studied to see if they have venomous bites – as are some other lizards, such as iguanas and legless lizards.

▶ Three-metre-long Komodo dragons are expert predators. They often wound prey with a vicious bite before stalking it and waiting for it to weaken.

Mammal bites and spurs

151 Of all the animal groups, mammals have the fewest venomous creatures. Most venomous mammals don't have venom strong enough to do much harm to people, apart from one kind – the duck-billed platypus of Australia.

Venomous spur

152 It is not known for definite why there are so few venomous mammals. Perhaps other animal groups, such as reptiles, evolved (developed) venom millions of years ago. Then new kinds of animals evolved from these original ancestors, and kept the ability to make venom. Venomous mammals evolved venom relatively recently.

153 Several kinds of shrews have venomous bites. They use the venom to disable and paralyze prey by biting hard and chewing with great speed. This is useful because shrews are very small, and often their prey is bigger and stronger than they are.

◄ The slow loris licks a poisonous fluid from glands on its elbows and then bites this into prey such as birds, moths and lizards.

▼ The male platypus' venom spur on the rear ankle is for self-defence rather than hunting for prey.

154 **The male platypus has a venomous spur on each rear foot.** It probably kicks out with this spur against enemies and predators, or against rival males in the breeding season. The venom can cause horrible pain and great swelling in humans, but it is not deadly.

▼ The Cuban solenodon grows almost as large as a pet cat! It uses its venomous saliva on prey such as spiders, worms and insects.

155 **Solenodons look rather like large shrews with long quivering noses, and they too have venom glands.** They deliver their venom using grooved teeth to bite into prey. There are only two kinds of solenodons, from the Caribbean islands of Cuba and Haiti (Hispaniola). They are both very rare.

Friends and enemies

156 Most venomous animals wander and hunt alone. But a few live in groups and help each other to catch prey and defend themselves. Social huntsman spiders live in groups of around 100. They gang up to attack large prey.

157 Many sea anemones allow certain sea creatures to live among their stinging tentacles. Clownfish have a special slimy body covering and also a bodily resistance, or immunity, to their anemone's venom. Some kinds of shrimps or prawns are protected by the anemone's tentacles, and in return they eat bits of leftover food to keep the anemone clean.

◄ This candy stripe shrimp is safe from the rose anemone's stings and can live among its tentacles. Different kinds of animals living together and helping each other like this is known as 'symbiosis'.

FRIENDLY ANEMONE

You will need:
hairdryer   tissue paper
card   sticky tape

Make an anemone by cutting strips of tissue paper and sticking them to a piece of card. By blowing on cold air from the hair dryer it will look as though the 'tentacles' are moving.

► The bonnethead, a type of hammerhead shark, can eat stingrays without suffering effects of the venom.

158 Some predators are resistant or immune to venom, even if it does get into their bodies. This is due to their body chemistry, which breaks down the venom quickly before it can do damage. Hammerhead sharks eat stingrays and even swallow their venomous spines, while kingsnakes are immune to rattlesnake venom – they attack and swallow them.

► The secretary bird relies on speed, agility and tough scales on its legs for protection as it stamps on venomous snakes to eat.

159 Even very venomous animals have enemies that attack and kill them for food. The mongoose and secretary bird kill and eat venomous snakes, and bee-eater birds catch bees and wasps. Usually the attacker has enough speed and skill to avoid being bitten or stung, as well as thick skin and fur or feathers for protection.

► The bee-eater bird holds its victim carefully in its hard beak and then rubs or bashes it on a branch or rock to get rid of the sting.

Most deadly

160 People are fascinated with venomous animals, and want to know which is the deadliest. But gathering serious scientific evidence to prove this is difficult and complicated. Experts continually make new discoveries about venomous animals, which change the 'most venomous' lists.

161 Some lists put together are from people who have been bitten or stung. But a snake or spider, for example, can bite and be gone in just a second. It is often very difficult to identify exactly which kind is responsible.

◀ Box jellyfish venom attacks the skin, nerves and heart within minutes. They have up to 60 tentacles, which can be over 3 metres long, and each has as many as 5000 stingers!

WANTED

▶ One of the most venomous animals, the stonefish of Southeast Asia and Australia is also one of the best camouflaged.

162 Other 'most venomous' lists are based on information recorded from real-life incidents. This takes into account how aggressive venomous animals are and how much venom they deliver in real-life situations. One problem with using this method is that some deaths are not reported, especially in remote areas.

▼ The death stalker scorpion has weak pincers and relies on its venom to kill prey.

163 Most venomous lists can also be affected by whether treatment exists. Before the 1980s, many people died from the bites of Sydney funnel-web spiders. Since the anti-venom was produced, there have been no known deaths, despite more bites reported. The funnel-web spider itself is just as venomous, and still bites people but it kills no one. Does the existence of an anti-venom reduce its deadliness?

WANTED

▼ Australia's inland taipan, almost 3 metres long, has the strongest venom of any snake – 200 times more powerful than that of a rattlesnake.

164 Many lists include some of the same animals. The box jellyfish, Brazilian wandering spider, death stalker scorpion, blue-ringed octopus, stonefish, Asian cobra, Russell's viper and inland taipan are all often contenders in most deadly venomous creature line-ups.

WANTED

Valuable venom

▲ Sydney funnel-web spiders can be tricked into oozing drops of venom from their fangs, which is then sucked up by a narrow glass tube

165 Scientists are discovering the incredible medical potential of venom. One example is bee venom – it may have anti-inflammatory substances, which can reduce swelling and pain. This method seems to work in some cases, but it's difficult to ensure the good effects whilst avoiding the bad, such as pain, swelling or allergic reactions.

▲ A scorpion is milked by stroking and massaging the tail end so its venom sprays or drips into a glass flask.

▲ People are checked to make sure they are not allergic to bee venom, before using it as possible treatment.

166 An anti-venom is a substance that works against a particular venom to reduce its harm. To develop anti-venoms, first the venom itself is obtained in pure form so scientists can study it. This is done by 'milking' the animal, making them eject their venom or by taking samples from dead animals.

▲ To milk a snake, it is encouraged to bite though a plastic sheet over a container so its venom seeps out.

QUIZ

QUIZ

Which of these exotic pets are venomous?

A. Chilean rose tarantula
B. Corn snake C. Iguana
D. Orange clownfish
E. Fuzzy dwarf lionfish
F. Atacama red pygmy scorpion

Answers:
A, E and F are venomous.

168 Some venomous animals are kept as pets. It's a dangerous hobby but keepers can help by studying the animals, their habits and how they behave. In turn, this helps conservation of rare venomous animals.

167 Studying venoms can lead to useful medicines and drugs. Scientists are testing substances in snake venom to treat strokes and some forms of cancers. Coneshell venom is being tested for many medical uses including painkilling drugs.

▼ Coneshells are kept in glass tanks of seawater so their venom can be collected when needed.

169 Through scientific research we can learn more about venomous animals. Discovering how and why animals use venom will allow us to reduce human suffering and protect the animals themselves, which are often killed. With more knowledge, hopefully fewer people will put themselves at risk, and venomous animals can exist without being feared or misunderstood.

SNAKES

170 **Snakes have lived on our planet for more than 120 million years.** There are nearly 3000 different species (type) of snake alive today. These spectacular, slithering serpents are superbly adapted to life without legs – the word 'serpent' means 'to creep'. Snakes are shy, secretive animals that avoid people whenever they can and will not usually attack unless they need to defend themselves.

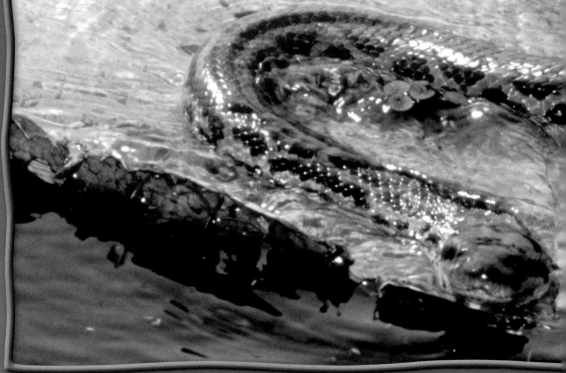

▶ The first snakes to evolve were constricting snakes, such as this huge anaconda, which squeezes its prey to death in its strong coils.

What is a snake?

171 **Snakes belong to the animal family group known as reptiles.** They are related to lizards, turtles, tortoises, crocodiles and alligators. Snakes may have evolved from swimming or burrowing lizards that lived millions of years ago, and are in fact very distant cousins of the dinosaurs!

172 **Snakes have long, thin bodies, with no legs, eyelids or external (outside) ears.** They can't blink, so they always seem to be staring. Some lizards also have no legs, but they do have eyelids and outer ears.

▼ More than three-quarters of snake species, such as this python, aren't poisonous.

REPTILE FAMILY

Over half of all reptiles are lizards – there are nearly 5000 species.

Amphisbaenians, or worm lizards, are burrowing reptiles that live underground.

Tuataras are rare, ancient and unusual reptiles from New Zealand.

Snakes are the second largest group of reptiles, after lizards. Hundreds of species of snakes are poisonous.

Crocodiles, alligators, gharials and caimans are predators with long, narrow snouts and sharp teeth.

Turtles and tortoises have a hard shell on their back, which protects them from predators.

173 **Like all reptiles, snakes are covered in waterproof scales.** A snake's scales grow in the top layers of its skin to protect its body as it slides over the ground. Scales allow skin to stretch when the snake moves or feeds.

TRUE OR FALSE?

1. Snakes have no eyelids.
2. A snake's tongue is shaped like a spoon.
3. Snakes need to eat five or six meals a day.

Answers:
1. True 2. False, it is shaped like a fork 3. False, snakes don't need to eat often and may eat only five or six meals in a year

▲ Snakes are most closely related to lizards, such as the Komodo dragon. It is the largest lizard in the world and can grow up to 3 metres in length.

174 A snake flicks its forked tongue in and out of its mouth regularly. The tongue is used to taste the air and pick up information about the snake's environment. Only a few animals have forked tongues – such as the Komodo dragon, and some other lizards.

175 All snakes are meat-eaters and swallow their prey whole. Since a snake's body works at a slow rate, it takes a long time to digest its food and so can survive for months without eating. A big snake in the wild may eat only five or six meals in a year.

▼ An African rock python opens its jaws extremely wide to swallow an impala, which is the size of a small deer.

Scaly skin

▲ Some snakes have 'keeled' scales, with a raised ridge along the middle of each scale.

176 A snake's skin is protected by a sheet of dry, horny scales that cover its body like a suit of armour. They are made from thick pieces of keratin – the substance that hair, feathers, nails and claws are made from. Snake scales are linked by hinges of thin keratin and usually fold back, overlapping each other.

Head scales

Ventral scales on the underside of the snake's body

Scutes

Dorsal scales on the sides and back

▶ The number, shape, colour and arrangment of a snake's scales helps with identification.

Subcaudal scales under the tail

Scale

Outer layer (epidermis)

Lower layer (dermis)

▲ The areas of skin between a snake's scales allow the body to stretch, making it very flexible.

177 Most snakes have a row of broad scales called scutes underneath their bodies. These scutes go across the snake's belly from one side to the other and end where the tail starts. They help the snake to grip the ground as it moves. Legless lizards don't have scutes, so this is one of the ways to tell them apart from snakes.

179 As snakes move and grow their skin becomes scratched and damaged. Adult snakes slough (moult) their outer layer of skin up to six times a year, but young snakes shed their skin more often as they are growing quickly.

178 The texture of a snake's scales helps it to move and catch prey. The scales of coral snakes and burrowing snakes are smooth. This helps them slide easily through small spaces. Wart snakes are covered with rough scales, which help them to grip slippery fish.

180 A snake's eyes are protected by clear, bubble-like scales. These 'spectacles' or 'brilles' cloud over before a snake sheds its skin. Snakes become sluggish and bad-tempered just before their skin peels off, which may be because they cannot see well and their skin is itchy.

▲ Fluid builds up between the old and new spectacles (scales that cover the eye).

▲ The outer skin peels back from the head and comes off inside out, revealing the new layer of skin that has grown underneath.

◀ The shed skin of a snake is stretched, making it longer than the snake it covered.

Colours and patterns

181 **Some snakes are brightly coloured to warn predators that they are poisonous.** There are more than 90 species of coral snake, each with a different pattern of red, black and yellow or white bands. Birds have learnt to avoid snakes with these warning colours.

▼ The bright tail of the ring-necked snake distracts predators away from its fragile head.

182 **Some snakes shimmer with rainbow colours.** Snakes in the sunbeam snake family are named after the way their large, smooth, polished scales create a rainbow effect along their bodies. As they move, light strikes the thin, see-through outer layers of their scales, making their colours appear to change.

◄ The scales of the rainbow boa glimmer with different colours.

SNAKE BRACELET

You will need:
thin card   scissors
colouring pencils   hole punch
wool   beads

Cut a strip of card 20 centimetres long and 3 centimetres wide. Use colouring pencils to draw a snake pattern on it. Punch a hole in each end of the card then tie together with strips of wool. Once you have threaded beads onto the wool and tied a knot in each end it is ready to wear.

183 Some snakes use bright colours to startle or threaten predators. Ring-necked snakes are dull colours on top but have brightly coloured bellies. If threatened, this snake will curl its tail into a corkscrew, creating a sudden flash of colour and drawing attention away from its vulnerable head.

◄ The extraordinary nose shield of the leaf-nosed snake may help to camouflage it while it hunts.

184 Many snakes have colours and patterns that make them blend into their surroundings. Their camouflage helps them avoid predators and catch their prey. Patterns on their scales help to break up the outline of their bodies. The patterns on a gaboon viper make it look just like the dead leaves on the floor of an African rainforest.

▼ The gaboon viper is well camouflaged among the leaves as it lies in wait for its prey.

On the move

185 **The way a snake moves depends on what species it is, its speed and the surface it is moving over.** A snake may wriggle along in an S-shape (serpentine movement), pull half of its body along at a time (concertina movement) or pull its body forwards in a straight line (caterpillar movement).

◄ Tree snakes use an adapted form of concertina movement to move from branch to branch.

186 **On smooth or sandy surfaces, snakes move by sidewinding.** By anchoring its head and tail firmly on a surface, it can fling the middle part of its body sideways. A sidewinding snake moves diagonally, with only a small part of its body touching the ground at any time.

▼ Sidewinding snakes, such as this viper, leave tracks at a 45° angle to the direction of travel.

187 **Tree snakes have strong, prehensile (gripping) tails, which coil around branches.** Holding on tightly with its tail, a tree snake stretches forwards to the next branch, and then pulls up its tail. This is a sort of concertina movement.

▲ Large, heavy snakes use their belly scutes to grip the ground and pull themselves forwards.

▲ Most snakes move in an S-shaped path, pushing forwards where their curves touch the ground.

▶ When using concertina movement, a snake bunches up its body (1) then stretches the front half forwards (2), and lastly, pulls up the back half of its body (3).

① ② ③

188

Sea snakes swim using S-shaped wriggles, rather like the serpentine movement used by many land snakes. To give them extra swimming power, sea snakes have broad, flat tails, which push against the water and propel them along.

▼ This high speed photo shows how a paradise tree snake flings its body into the air from a branch to glide for distances of up to 100 metres.

189

A few Asian tree snakes glide through the trees by spreading out their long ribs to create a sort of parachute. This slows down the snakes' fall, so that they float from tree to tree instead of plummeting straight down to the ground.

Super senses

190 Snakes rely on their senses of smell, taste and touch much more than sight or hearing. A snake's tongue is used to collect particles from the air and to touch and feel its surroundings. A snake has a special nerve pit called the Jacobson's organ in the roof of its mouth, which analyses tastes and smells collected by its tongue.

▲ A snake can flick its tongue in and out through a tiny opening even when its mouth is closed. An active snake will do this every few seconds, especially when it is hunting or feels threatened.

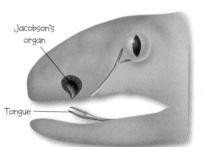

Jacobson's organ

Tongue

◀ A snake's tongue collects scent particles and chemicals from the air and places them in the two openings of the Jacobson's organ in the roof of its mouth.

QUIZ

1. What is the name of the sense organ in the roof of a snake's mouth?

2. What shape are the pupils of snakes that hunt at night?

3. Why do boas and pythons need to sense heat?

Answers:
1. Jacobson's organ 2. Vertical slits
3. They need to detect the warm bodies of their prey

191 Most snakes have well-developed eyes and some have good eyesight. Some tree snakes have a groove along the snout in front of each of their eyes, so they can see forwards to judge depth and distance. Coachwhip snakes are one of the few snakes to hunt mainly by sight, raising the front end parts of their bodies off the ground.

192 Day-hunting snakes usually have round pupils, whereas night-hunting snakes have vertical, slit-shaped pupils. Vertical pupils can be closed more tightly than round ones, helping protect the snake's eyes from bright light when it comes out to bask in the Sun during the day.

▶ The day-hunting oriental whip snake has a distinctive keyhole-shaped pupil.

▶ The round pupil of a Natal green snake is surrounded by a beautiful golden iris.

▼ By looking along grooves in its narrow, pointed snout, a vine snake can focus both eyes at once, giving it 3D vision.

▶ The eyelash viper has the typical slit-shaped pupil of a night-hunting snake.

193 Snakes have no outer ears or eardrums so they cannot hear sounds in the same way we do. They have an inner ear bone connected to the jaw, which helps them to sense ground vibrations. A snake can also pick up vibrations from the air through its skin.

Heat pits

194 Some snakes, such as pit vipers, boas and pythons, are able to sense the heat given off by their prey. They are the only animals that can do this and their unique sense allows them to track warm-blooded prey, such as rats, in the dark.

◀ Vipers have holes behind their nostrils that are lined with heat-sensitive cells. Boas and pythons have similar heat holes along their lips.

Hunting and eating

195 Most snakes eat a wide variety of prey depending on their size, the season and what is available. But a few snakes have very specific diets. Thirst snakes feed only on slugs and snails, queen snakes eat crayfish and children's pythons can move fast enough to catch bats.

▶ The common kingsnake can eat poisonous snakes. It can digest the venom so it is not harmed.

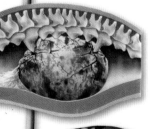

◀ The jaws of an egg–eating snake stretch to swallow an egg three times the diameter of its head.

◀ Once the egg has been swallowed, the snake arches its neck, forcing pointed bones in its throat to break through the shell.

196 An egg–eating snake swallows eggs whole and uses the pointed ends of bones that jut into its throat to crack open the shell. Eggs are a useful source of food because they are rich in body-building protein as well as being easy to find.

◀ The snake then swallows the egg's nutritious contents, and regurgitates (coughs up) the crushed eggshell.

I DON'T BELIEVE IT!

Large snakes can swallow prey up to a quarter of their own length. They have been known to eat leopards, gazelles and even small crocodiles!

198 Many snakes lie in wait to ambush their prey because they cannot move fast enough to chase after it. Snakes such as vipers, boas and pythons have wide bodies so they can eat big meals. They do not have breastbones, so they can move their ribs apart at the front to make their bodies even wider.

199 Some snakes, such as the king cobra, even eat other snakes! A snake's body is easier to swallow than other prey, such as mammals or birds, because it is a thin, smooth shape. Most snakes that eat poisonous snakes are immune to their poisons.

197 Some snakes set traps for their prey. The death adder has a brightly coloured tip to its tail, which looks similar to a worm. The adder wriggles this 'worm' to lure lizards, birds and worms within reach of its poisonous jaws.

▼ Young Mexican cantils have a bright green or yellow tip to their tail. They use this to lure prey, such as frogs, lizards or rodents.

Teeth and jaws

200 **Most snakes have short, sharp, curved teeth to grip and hold their prey.** The teeth are no good for chewing or tearing up food, which is why snakes swallow their prey whole. A snake's teeth often break as it feeds, but new teeth grow to replace broken ones.

SNAKE BITE!

Snakes want to be left alone. If you see a snake, remain calm, don't panic, keep still and quiet and let the snake go its own way.

When out hiking in areas where snakes live, look where you are going, wear tall boots or hard shoes and don't disturb piles of debris or dark holes.

Never try to pick up a snake — it may bite or spit venom if it feels threatened.

Be aware of how to call for professional help in an emergency and if possible carry an anti-venom kit.

201 **Many smaller snakes swallow prey alive, but larger snakes kill their food before they eat it.** Around 700 species of snakes use poison, called venom, to immobilize or kill their prey. The venom is injected into the prey through large, pointed teeth, called fangs, which are connected to glands (bags) of venom in the snake's head.

▶ Rear-fanged snakes need to chew their venom into their prey for 15 minutes or more before the poison takes effect.

202 **Snakes can have fangs at the front or back of their mouths.** Some fanged snakes, such as vipers and cobras, have fangs at the front, while a few snakes, such as the African boomslang, have fangs at the back. Back fangs may either just be large back teeth, or they may have grooves for venom.

▼ Fangs at the back of a snake's mouth help to kill prey as it is being swallowed.

Fangs are towards the rear of the mouth, below the eye

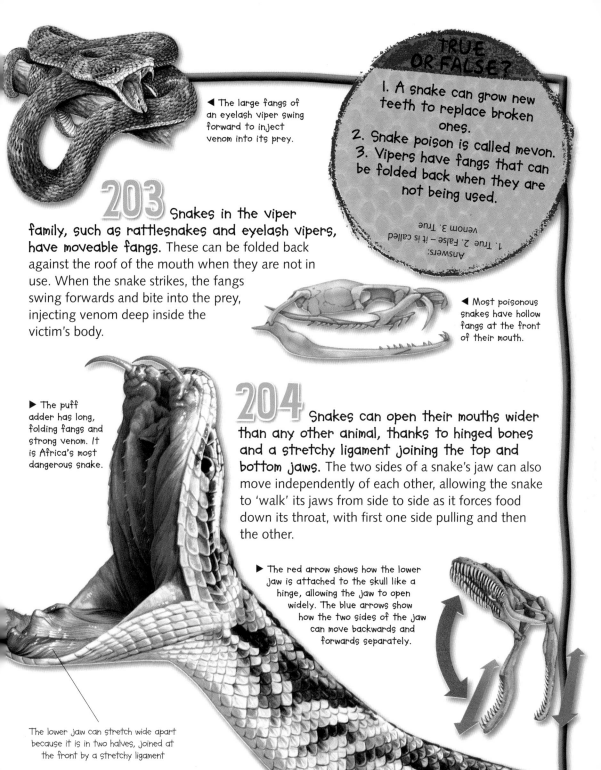

◄ The large fangs of an eyelash viper swing forward to inject venom into its prey.

203 Snakes in the viper family, such as rattlesnakes and eyelash vipers, have moveable fangs. These can be folded back against the roof of the mouth when they are not in use. When the snake strikes, the fangs swing forwards and bite into the prey, injecting venom deep inside the victim's body.

◄ Most poisonous snakes have hollow fangs at the front of their mouth.

► The puff adder has long, folding fangs and strong venom. It is Africa's most dangerous snake.

204 Snakes can open their mouths wider than any other animal, thanks to hinged bones and a stretchy ligament joining the top and bottom jaws. The two sides of a snake's jaw can also move independently of each other, allowing the snake to 'walk' its jaws from side to side as it forces food down its throat, with first one side pulling and then the other.

► The red arrow shows how the lower jaw is attached to the skull like a hinge, allowing the jaw to open widely. The blue arrows show how the two sides of the jaw can move backwards and forwards separately.

The lower jaw can stretch wide apart because it is in two halves, joined at the front by a stretchy ligament

Poisonous snakes

205
Venom is a highly modified form of saliva (spit). Saliva is a type of digestive juice, so venom contains enzymes (particles that break down food). These start to digest and soften the meal even before the snake has swallowed it. Snakes don't run out of venom, because their glands make more poison as they use it up.

▶ Eyelash vipers catch prey while hanging from tree branches. Small animals are overcome by venom in minutes.

VENOM KEY

① Venom gland sits in the side of the snake's head

② A tube leads from the gland down to the fangs

③ Fangs are hollow with a venom canal down the middle

④ Venom is injected deep into the prey's muscle tissue

206
Snake venom is a complicated substance that works in two main ways. Snakes such as cobras, coral snakes and sea snakes have venom that attacks the victim's nervous system, causing paralysis (stopping all movement) and preventing breathing. Snakes such as vipers have venom that destroys body tissues, particularly attacking the circulatory system (blood vessels) and muscles.

207 Venom is useful because it allows snakes to overcome their prey quickly without being injured. Snakes with powerful venom, such as vipers, tend to bite their prey quickly and then retreat to a place of safety while their poison takes effect. If the victim crawls away to die, the snake follows its scent trail to keep track of its meal.

▲ The venom of the common krait is very powerful – these snakes are even more poisonous than common cobras.

▼ As the snake bites down, venom flows down its fangs and can be collected in the bottom of a jar.

208 If a person is bitten by a venomous snake the deadliness of the bite varies. The size and health of the victim, the size of the snake, the number of bites, the amount of venom injected and the speed and quality of medical treatment are important. Some of the most dangerous snakes in the world are the black mamba, Russell's viper and the beaked sea snake.

▶ The black mamba is the longest venomous snake in Africa and is named after the black colour inside its mouth, which it displays if threatened.

209 Venom is collected from poisonous snakes by making them bite down on the top of a jar. The venom is used to make a medicine called antivenom, which helps people recover from snake bites. Snake venom can also be used to make other medicines that treat high blood pressure, heart failure and kidney disease.

I DON'T BELIEVE IT!
The king cobra is the world's longest venomous snake, growing to lengths of over 5.4 metres. Its venom is powerful enough to kill an elephant!

95

Cobras and vipers

210 **The two main groups of poisonous snakes are vipers and elapids.** The cobras of Africa and Asia belong to the elapid family, as do the colourful coral snakes of the Americas and the mambas of Africa. Elapids have short, fixed fangs at the front of their mouths, as do their relatives, the sea snakes.

211 **Cobras can spread out the skin around their neck into a wide 'hood' that makes them look larger and frightening to their attackers.** The hood is supported by long, movable ribs in the cobra's neck. Some cobras have huge eye-spots on the back of the hood, which probably startle predators.

212 **To defend themselves, spitting cobras spray venom through small slits in the tips of their fangs.** They aim for the eyes of an attacker and can spit venom for distances of up to 1.8 metres – the height of a tall man.

◄ Cobras follow the movement of a snake charmer's pipe. They cannot actually hear the music.

▼ Spitting cobras spray their venom by pushing air out of their lungs while forcing the venom through holes in the front of their fangs.

213 The viper family of venomous snakes includes the adders, night adders, vipers, bush vipers, rattlesnakes, copperheads, asps and pit vipers. All vipers have long, hollow fangs that can be folded back inside their mouths. The largest viper is the bushmaster, which lives in the forests of Central and South America and grows up to 3.6 metres in length.

▼ The palm viper lives in trees and shrubs, often at the base of palm fronds. Its prehensile tail acts as an anchor.

214 The puff adder inflates its lungs when threatened, which makes its body puff up like a balloon, making it look bigger than it really is. The saw-scaled viper is also named after its threat display because it makes a rasping sound with its jagged-edged scales.

Crushing coils

215 Snakes that squeeze their prey to death by wrapping it tightly in their strong coils are called constrictors. All boas and pythons are constrictors, as are the sunbeam snakes and some of the snakes in the colubrid family, such as rat snakes and kingsnakes.

▼ 1. The snake holds its prey in its teeth and squeezes it to death in its strong coils.

▲ 2. When the animal is dead, the snake opens its mouth very wide and starts to swallow its meal.

216 Constricting snakes usually hold the head end of their prey with their sharp teeth. They then throw their coils around the animal's body and squeeze hard to stop it from breathing. Each time the victim breathes out, the snake squeezes a little harder, until it dies from suffocation or shock.

217
The time it takes for the snake's prey to die depends on the size of the prey and how strong it is. When the prey stops struggling, the snake relaxes its grip, unhinges its jaws and starts to force its meal down its throat.

218
Prey is usually swallowed head-first. The legs or wings of the animal fold back against the sides of the body and the fur or feathers lie flat – making it easier for the snake to swallow. Slimy saliva in the snake's mouth helps the prey to slide down its throat and into its stomach.

219
When it is swallowing a large meal, a snake finds it difficult to breathe. It may take a long time to swallow a big animal. The snake moves the opening of its windpipe to the front of its mouth so that it can keep breathing while it swallows.

▼ 3. A snake's meal forms a bulge in the middle of its body while it is being digested. It may take days, or even weeks, to be absorbed completely.

Boas and pythons

220 Two powerful types of constricting snakes are boas and pythons. Unlike many other types of snake, most of them have a working left lung, hip bones and the remains of back leg bones. Many boas and pythons have heat-sensitive jaw pits to detect their prey.

221 Many boas and pythons have markings that give them excellent camouflage. The patterns help them to lie in wait for their prey without being seen. The sand boa perfectly matches the rocks and sand of its desert habitat.

▲ The shape of the Kenyan sand boa's mouth and jaws helps it to dig through soft sand.

222 The ball python, or royal python, from West Africa, coils into a tight ball when it is threatened. Its head is well protected in the middle of its coils and it can even be rolled along the ground in this position.

▶ A ball python in a defensive ball shows off its camouflage colours. These snakes can live for up to 50 years.

223 **The emerald tree boa and the green tree python look alike.** These two snakes live in different parts of the world and are not closely related, but they look and act in a similar way because they both live in rainforest environments.

Emerald tree boa

▲▼ Emerald tree boas and green tree pythons rest in the same way, coiled around branches. They grip tightly with their prehensile tails.

224 **Boas and pythons live in different places around the world.** Most boas live in Central and South America, while pythons live in Africa, southeast Asia and Australia. Another difference between the two snake groups is that all boas (except for one species) give birth to live young, while all pythons lay eggs.

I DON'T BELIEVE IT!
The smallest type of python in the world is the anthill python, which grows to a maximum length of 30 centimetres.

Green tree python

BIRDS OF PREY

225 Birds of prey are magnificent hunters of the sky. They soar through the air using their large wings to keep them aloft, as they scan the ground below for food. Some birds of prey, such as eagles, are hunters and kill to eat. Others, such as vultures, eat carrion (dead animals). Birds of prey are also called raptors, from the Latin *rapere*, meaning to grab or seize, because they kill with their feet.

▼ A long-legged buzzard brings food to its chicks. These birds of prey nest on cliff ledges and feed on small mammals, reptiles and large insects.

Eagle-eyed predators

226 Like all hunters, birds of prey need to be kitted out with tools. They have sharp senses, muscular bodies, tough beaks and grasping feet with sharp talons. They can detect prey from great distances and launch deadly attacks with skill and accuracy. Some can fly at super speeds.

▼ Golden eagles are large birds, measuring about 2 metres from wing tip to wing tip.

Finger-like primary flight feathers at wing tips

Rusty brown feathers

227 Raptors are able to fly high above the ground. The sky not only offers a great view of prey, it is also a safe place for birds as they search. As adults, birds of prey do have natural enemies, but even on land they are usually a match for most other predators due to their size.

228 Good eyesight is essential for raptors. They need to be able to locate prey that is in grass or under cover, often from a great distance. Birds of prey have eyes that are packed with light-detecting cells. The eyes are positioned near the front of the head, which means a bird can see well in front, to the side and partly around to the back.

▼ Birds of prey have large eyes that face forwards, to give them excellent vision.

The area of binocular vision

Peripheral vision

There is only a small 'blind area' behind the bird

QUIZ

Which of these animals are predators and which are prey?

Leopard Warthog
Eagle Crocodile
Tortoise Wildebeest

Answers:
Predators: leopard, eagle, crocodile
Prey: warthog, tortoise, wildebeest

229 **Birds of prey have big, powerful bodies.**
This helps them catch and kill food, but means they
need more energy to fly. Meat is an energy-
packed food, ideal for building muscles.
Even the largest birds of prey can
swoop and soar, although
smaller birds are usually
more acrobatic in flight.

Pale feathers on crown

White–tailed eagle
Large, heavy bill

Large, broad
wings

► Eagles and vultures have big,
tough bills, but falcons have
smaller, sharp bills. A bird's bill
and talons are made of a hard
substance called keratin, the
same as our nails.

Large bill

Large tail

Egyptian vulture
Long, hooked bill

Powerful feet with
sharp talons

Birds of prey may carry
their food to a safe
place to eat it, but
others eat their prey
where it was killed

230 **Scientists used to think
that all birds of prey had a poor
sense of smell.** The turkey vulture is the only bird of
prey known to have a good sense of smell, and probably
the only one able to smell out its food. They can detect
carrion on the ground while they are flying.

Gyrfalcon
Short bill with
a sharp hook

Hovering and soaring

231 Birds of prey have one advantage over most other predators – they can fly. Flying allows creatures to escape from other animals and stay safe. They can explore new areas easily as they search for food, mates or places to breed.

232 Birds' bodies are perfectly adapted for flying. They have light bones that are mostly hollow, but still strong. Their big hearts and lungs can collect lots of oxygen with every breath. This is the gas that animals need to turn their food into energy.

Skull

Humerus – similar to our upper arm bone

Keel – where large flight muscles are attached

Narrow, pointed wings

Metacarpals – form a 'hand'

Wingbeats are stiff and shallow

Ribs

▶ Hovering and flying require lots of energy, so kestrels have light bodies with muscles and powerful wings. Their skeleton is very light and flexible, but also strong and rigid.

The long tail feathers are spread out to keep the bird steady while it is hovering, looking for food

I DON'T BELIEVE IT!

Hobbies are amongst the fastest, most acrobatic fliers of all. They can dive, twist and turn, bombing towards the ground at great speeds, only opening their wings a few metres above the ground.

233 Kestrels hover and look as if they are hardly moving. They fly facing the wind, staying in the same spot above the ground. Kestrels spread their tails and the feathers at their wing tips turn up, which helps them to stay steady. As they lower their heads, they get a good view of the ground and any small animals, before launching an attack.

234
Birds of prey with long, broad wings soar through the sky. They also have large, fan-shaped tails that, with their wings, catch the air like a parachute. Soaring birds, such as eagles and vultures, often wait until the air is warm before they fly. As air is heated by the Sun it rises. Large, soaring birds use these flows of warm air, called thermal uplifts, to get airborne and rise high above the ground.

As ground air is heated, it becomes lighter

Lighter, warmer air rises, creating thermals

Thermals help big birds fly high and soar

▲ Thermals are hot air currents that travel upwards. Birds of prey use them to reach greater heights.

235
At breeding time, male birds of prey often perform display flights. These might help to attract females or mark out territory. There are different patterns of display flights, from circling round and round, to dive bombing or swooping up and down.

▶ At mating time, one golden eagle dives towards its mate, which turns its back, and they wrestle one another with their feet.

Hunting weapons

236 Predators need good senses to find prey, speed to catch it and weapons for killing it. Raptors are equipped with bodies that are ideal for locating and killing, but learning the skills to hunt takes time, patience and practice.

237 The most important weapons are feet and mouths. Raptors' bills are usually hooked, with a pointed tip. Birds that hunt other birds, such as falcons, hawks and owls, often have short, hooked bills. Those raptors that hunt larger animals need long, strong bills.

◀ Tawny owls have soft feathers that muffle noise, so they can take off in silence.

▼ This golden eagle's toes have dagger-like claws (talons) that can pierce flesh with ease.

238 Raptors' feet have talons and they are highly developed for hunting. Each foot has three strong, scaly toes at the front and one at the side or back. When the toes are bent they can grasp like a hand – perfect for holding wriggling prey.

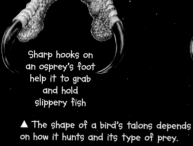

Sharp hooks on an osprey's foot help it to grab and hold slippery fish

When a barn owl grabs its prey, its foot can spread wide to get a good grip

A black vulture does not need very sharp talons, as it usually feeds on carrion

▲ The shape of a bird's talons depends on how it hunts and its type of prey.

239 Feet give clues about how a bird hunts. Birds of prey with short legs and short feet usually kill on the ground. Birds with long legs, long feet and slender, sharp talons catch and kill their prey in the air. Birds with especially big hind toes grab hold of large animals, such as rabbits or even deer.

▶ Rapid wingbeats can change the owl's direction easily.

240 Tawny owls mostly hunt at night. They wait on a perch, looking and listening for small animals that may be moving around nearby. They sometimes beat their wings to startle other perching birds, forcing them into flight. Once the birds are in the air, the owls can follow their movements and prepare to attack. They can even pick birds or bats off their perches or out of nests.

▶ As they prepare to grab their prey, tawny owls spread their wings to cover it and they kill it instantly with their bill and feet.

Fussy eaters

241 **Some birds of prey have unusual diets.** Lesser spotted eagles that live around wetlands feast on frogs. Snail kites have curved, hooked bills for extracting snails from their shells. Palm-nut vultures eat the fruits of palm trees.

▲ When ospreys plunge into water, they close their nostrils so the water doesn't shoot up into their nose. They carry their catch back to the nest to eat in peace or feed it to their chicks.

▶ Snail kites live in South American wetlands and eat water snails, turtles and crabs. They also hunt rodents, such as rats and mice.

242 **Plucking a fish out of water takes huge skill.** Yet some birds of prey can achieve this incredible feat. They soar over water, watching for movement at the surface. Once they have spied a fish, the birds dive down and plunge their feet into the water to grab it. This requires sharp eyesight, quick reactions and an agile body.

243 **Ospreys are fish–eaters.** These birds of prey nest near lakes and rivers or by clean, calm coastal areas. They hover up to 30 metres above the water until they spot a fish. Then they dive down with half-closed wings and stretch out their legs and feet just before hitting the water.

244 White-tailed eagles pluck both fish and ducks out of the water. They perch on trees and swoop down to grab prey. Sharp growths, called spicules, on the feet help to grip wet prey and large bills are ideal for ripping and tearing flesh.

245 Lammergeiers eat a diet of bones and scraps left behind by other predators. They pick up large bones with their feet and fly to a height of 80 metres before dropping the bones to the ground to split them. These birds also drop tortoises to get to the soft flesh inside the shell.

FISH EATERS

Penguins are flightless birds that catch fish to eat. Find out where they live and how they catch fish. How are their bodies different to those of birds of prey?

▶ If a bone is dropped from a great height it splits open. The lammergeier can then eat the soft marrow inside.

111

Snake stampers

Black flight feathers

Black crest feathers

246 **Secretary birds are not like other raptors.** They are tall, elegant and long-legged. These birds stride through the long grasses of African plains, looking for insects and other animals to eat. When they find their prey, they stamp and peck it to death.

Grey plumage on body

247 Secretary birds eat snakes, even poisonous ones, such as cobras and adders. When it spies a snake in the vegetation, a secretary bird runs towards it and stamps on it, or inflicts a kick to the head. A sharp peck to the back of the snake's neck finishes it off. If the prey proves too tough to kill this way, the bird may grab it in its beak, take to the skies and drop it from a great height.

Large feet

Long legs

▶ A male secretary bird can grow to about 1.4 metres tall. Secretary birds might get their name from the crest of long, black quill feathers on their heads, which look like old-fashioned ink pens.

248 Snakes are no match for a secretary bird. These predators run fast during a chase and their legs are covered in thick scales to protect them from bites. If a snake fights back, the secretary bird spreads its wings to form a shield. The flapping wings scare the snake and if it bites a feather, the bird will suffer no harm. They often hunt in pairs and can walk more than 25 kilometres every day in search of food.

QUIZ

1. How tall can a male secretary bird grow to be?
2. What are secretary birds' legs covered in?
3. How many snakes does a family of short-toed eagles need every day?

Answers:
1. About 1.4 metres
2. Thick scales 3. At least five

249 When they are angry, excited or scared, secretary birds raise their quill feathers. Their body feathers are grey and white, but black feathers at the top of their long legs make them appear as if they are wearing short trousers! Males and females look similar, but females are smaller.

▶ Short-toed eagles feed dead snakes to their young, which have enormous appetites.

250 Not many birds of prey eat snakes, but short-toed eagles eat almost nothing else. They attack snakes that are nearly 2 metres long and even eat poisonous ones. A family of short-toed eagles needs at least five snakes every day, so the adults spend a lot of time hunting their slithery prey.

Eagles

251 Eagles are large, heavy-bodied birds with strong legs, big bills and feet, and broad wings. They are usually smaller than vultures, but larger than most other birds of prey. There are about 60 types, including fish eagles, snake eagles, harpy eagles and hawk eagles.

252 These birds live in all regions of the world except Antarctica. Golden eagles are one of the most common, widespread types. There may be as many as one million and they live in North America, Europe and Asia, around mountains, forests and cliffs. The Great Nicobar serpent eagle is a rare eagle. It lives on one small island near India, and there may be fewer than 1000.

▼ Large birds of prey, such as eagles, rely on thermals to reach height in the sky.

2 An eagle uses thermals to reach a good height for spotting its prey, and then swoops.

1 Warm air thermals travel upwards.

253 Eagles are not as agile as some other birds of prey. When they hunt, they are more likely to soar and stoop than to hover and dive. Eagles often perch to watch for prey, then swoop in low for the kill.

4 The eagle flies off with its prey held firmly in its feet.

3 As the bird flies towards its prey, it swings its feet forward to grab hold of it.

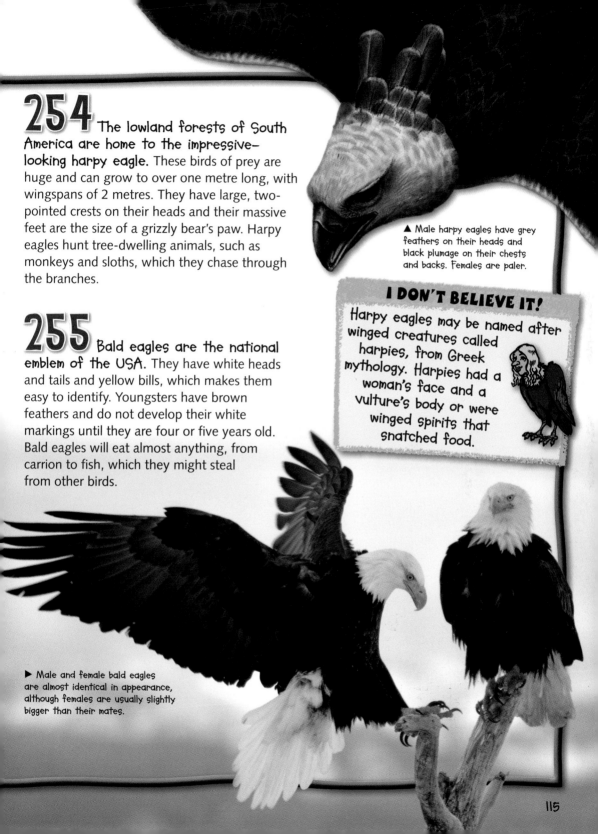

254 The lowland forests of South America are home to the impressive-looking harpy eagle. These birds of prey are huge and can grow to over one metre long, with wingspans of 2 metres. They have large, two-pointed crests on their heads and their massive feet are the size of a grizzly bear's paw. Harpy eagles hunt tree-dwelling animals, such as monkeys and sloths, which they chase through the branches.

▲ Male harpy eagles have grey feathers on their heads and black plumage on their chests and backs. Females are paler.

255 Bald eagles are the national emblem of the USA. They have white heads and tails and yellow bills, which makes them easy to identify. Youngsters have brown feathers and do not develop their white markings until they are four or five years old. Bald eagles will eat almost anything, from carrion to fish, which they might steal from other birds.

I DON'T BELIEVE IT!
Harpy eagles may be named after winged creatures called harpies, from Greek mythology. Harpies had a woman's face and a vulture's body or were winged spirits that snatched food.

▶ Male and female bald eagles are almost identical in appearance, although females are usually slightly bigger than their mates.

Kites and buzzards

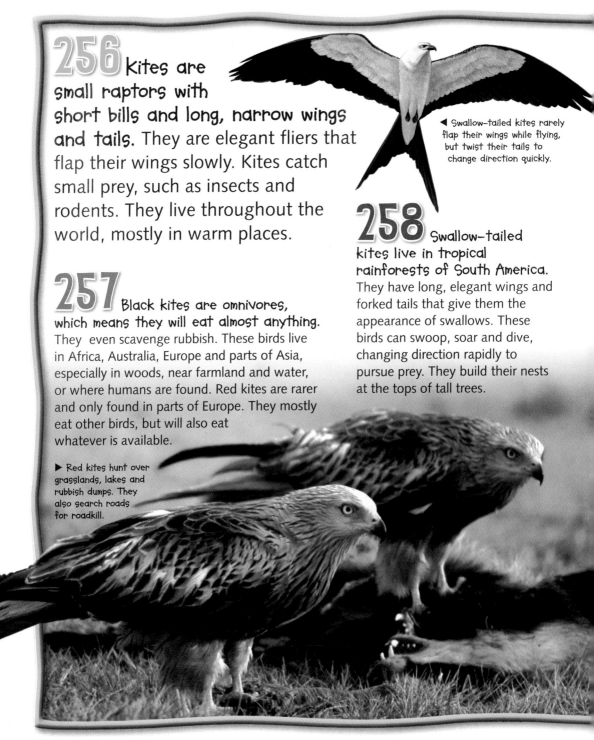

256 Kites are small raptors with short bills and long, narrow wings and tails. They are elegant fliers that flap their wings slowly. Kites catch small prey, such as insects and rodents. They live throughout the world, mostly in warm places.

◀ Swallow-tailed kites rarely flap their wings while flying, but twist their tails to change direction quickly.

257 Black kites are omnivores, which means they will eat almost anything. They even scavenge rubbish. These birds live in Africa, Australia, Europe and parts of Asia, especially in woods, near farmland and water, or where humans are found. Red kites are rarer and only found in parts of Europe. They mostly eat other birds, but will also eat whatever is available.

▶ Red kites hunt over grasslands, lakes and rubbish dumps. They also search roads for roadkill.

258 Swallow-tailed kites live in tropical rainforests of South America. They have long, elegant wings and forked tails that give them the appearance of swallows. These birds can swoop, soar and dive, changing direction rapidly to pursue prey. They build their nests at the tops of tall trees.

259
Buzzards are big-bodied birds with broad wings and large, rounded tails. When they fly, they beat their wings slowly and gracefully. They eat small mammals and insects. Honey buzzards eat wasps and bees. They rip open hives with their talons and bills, then eat the larvae, pupae and adult insects. These birds have slit-like nostrils and bristles instead of feathers between their eyes, which may protect them from stings.

260
In the Americas, buzzards are often called hawks. Swainson's hawk spends summer in the USA and travels to South America for winter. When breeding, they eat mice, squirrels and reptiles, but for the rest of the year they survive mostly on insects, such as grasshoppers and beetles. They often walk along the ground looking for food and sometimes hunt in teams.

◀ A common buzzard feeds during winter. There are nearly 30 species (types) of buzzards and they belong to a group of raptors called Buteos.

QUIZ
1. Which kites have the appearance of swallows?
2. Which buzzards eat wasps and bees?
3. Which hawk sometimes hunts in teams?

Answers:
1. Swallow-tailed kites
2. Honey buzzards
3. Swainson's hawk

Fast falcons

▶ A peregrine falcon pursues a swallow. It has recently been discovered that peregrines that live in towns are able to hunt at night, helped by city lights to find their prey.

261 A peregrine falcon can move faster than any other animal on Earth. These birds reach speeds of 100 kilometres an hour when chasing prey. When peregrines stoop from heights of one kilometre and plummet through the sky, they may reach speeds of 300 kilometres an hour or more.

262 Peregrines are travellers and have one of the longest migrations of any raptors. American peregrines have been known to cover 25,000 kilometres in just one year. These raptors are the most widespread of all birds of prey and live on every continent except Antarctica, but they are rare.

▼ Saker falcons have bold markings while some Eleonora's falcons have rusty pink breast feathers.

Eleonora's falcon

Saker falcon

263 There are about 35 species of falcon and most of them are speedy fliers. They are medium-sized raptors with muscle-packed bodies, pointed wings and short tails. They usually nest in cliffs and lay several eggs at a time. Falcons prey upon birds and other small animals.

I DON'T BELIEVE IT!

At breeding time, female gyrfalcons often store food near the nest. They are able to break off frozen bits of food with their bills.

▶ Gyrfalcons are bulky birds with extra body fat that helps them to keep warm.

264 Gyrfalcons can cope with the cold and they live around the Earth's frozen north. Some gyrfalcons are brown or grey. The further north they live, the paler they become, so they are camouflaged against the snowy landscape. These are the biggest falcons, with a wingspan of up to 1.3 metres, so they can pursue large prey such as ptarmigans, gulls and geese.

▼ Lesser kestrels spend the winters in Africa, travelling into Europe for the summer. They mostly feed on insects, but in spring they hunt reptiles and small mammals.

265 Kestrels are types of falcon that hover before attacking their prey. These small birds of prey have rounded heads and large eyes. While male and female raptors often have the same colour plumage, male kestrels are usually more colourful than the females.

Hawks and harriers

▼ Goshawks live in forested areas of Europe. They mainly hunt birds that are weak or ill because sick animals make easier targets.

266 Hawks, sparrowhawks and goshawks belong to a group of raptors called Accipiters. They are medium-sized birds and live in forests and woodlands. Short, rounded wings and long tails help them to fly in short bursts between trees, darting through branches in pursuit of small mammals and birds.

267 Most hawks hunt rodents, such as rats. They are useful because they eat pests that damage crops. However goshawks hunt game birds and poultry. Game birds, such as pheasants, are bred by farmers to be hunted for sport. Poultry, such as chickens, are an important food for humans. Goshawks have been killed to stop them from hunting these birds.

I DON'T BELIEVE IT!
Sharp-shinned hawks of America take their prey to a special perch called a butcher's block. This is where the raptor plucks all the feathers or fur off its prey, so these bits don't mess up its nest!

268

Hawks may squeeze their prey to death. Many raptors use their feet to hold prey and their bills to kill it. Cooper's hawks hold a captured animal with their sharp talons and fly with it until it dies. They have been known to hold prey underwater to drown it.

▶ Hawks have rounded heads with short bills. Their compact bodies help them to fly fast and change direction.

270

Harriers are raptors that look similar to hawks, with long legs and tails. They often fly low over fields and meadows, scouring the ground for snakes, frogs, insects, small birds or mammals. Hen harriers live in Europe, Asia and North America, but the populations of birds on each side of the Atlantic are slightly different from one another. North American birds are usually called marsh harriers or northern harriers.

Common black hawks live near water in Central America

Red-tailed hawks of North America inhabit woods, deserts and mountains

269

Eurasian sparrowhawks are one of the most common raptors in the world. They live in forests, farms, woods and parks across Europe and Asia during the spring and summer, and travel south for the winter. Despite being common, sparrowhawks are so secretive that they are rarely seen. However when food is scarce they may investigate gardens, searching for song birds such as sparrows to eat.

Eurasian sparrowhawks hide their nests in woodlands

Hunters of the night

271 **Most owls hunt at night.** As well as having talons and sharp bills, owls have big eyes that face the front and can see depth and movement. Eyes have two types of cells – one detecting colours, the other just faint or dim light. Some owls only have light-detecting cells and can see in the darkness, but not colour.

272 **Owls use feathers to help them hear and to stop animals from hearing them.** Their ears are covered by feathers that direct sound into the ear canal. Downy feathers on the body and feet help to soften sound as the bird moves. Feathers on the wings are arranged in a way that deadens the sound of flapping, so the bird descends silently on its prey.

▲ Like some other owls, this great horned owl is nocturnal, which means that it is most active at night. It begins hunting at dusk and settles down to sleep when the Sun rises.

◄ Owls have three eyelids. The third eyelid is a special membrane that sweeps over the eye to clean it.

▶ Pellets can be opened and their contents studied to discover the diet of a bird of prey.

Pellet from a little owl

Pellet from a long-eared owl

Pellet from a barn owl

Pellet from a red kite

275 Owls eat a range of food, including insects, birds, bats and fish, and they often swallow an animal whole. Like other birds of prey, owls are not able to digest the hard parts of a body, such as bones, fur or feathers. They bring them up from their stomach and spit them out in the form of pellets. It takes about seven hours for one pellet to form.

273 Eurasian eagle owls have a wingspan of nearly 2 metres. The largest owls, they attack other birds to steal their territories. Tiny elf owls catch their prey in flight. They are the smallest owls, with a wingspan of just 15 centimetres.

274 Many birds of prey build their own nests, but owls do not. They either use old nests left by other birds, or they lay their eggs in a hole in a tree, a hollow in the ground or inside an abandoned building. Owls usually lay a clutch of up to seven eggs at a time and the chicks are called owlets.

▶ Tawny owls nest in tree hollows. They lay 2–6 eggs and the fluffy chicks do not leave the nest until they are about 35 days old.

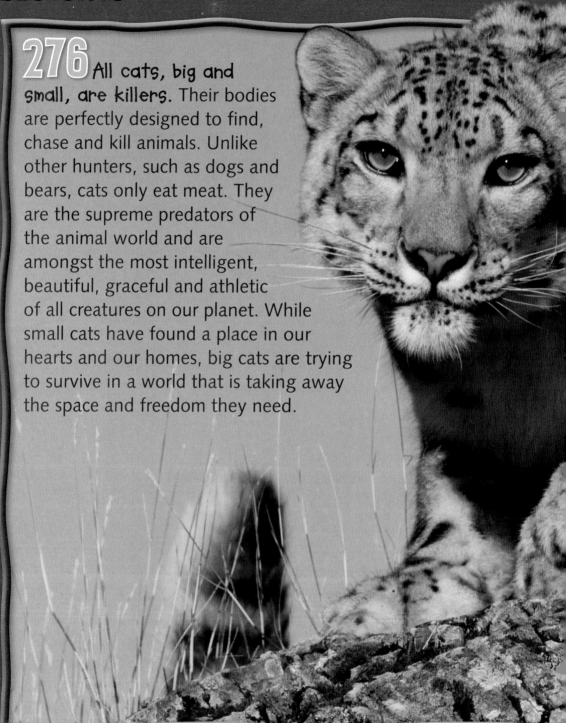

BIG CATS

276 **All cats, big and small, are killers.** Their bodies are perfectly designed to find, chase and kill animals. Unlike other hunters, such as dogs and bears, cats only eat meat. They are the supreme predators of the animal world and are amongst the most intelligent, beautiful, graceful and athletic of all creatures on our planet. While small cats have found a place in our hearts and our homes, big cats are trying to survive in a world that is taking away the space and freedom they need.

◀ The snow leopard roams a mountainous area of Central Asia where the weather is cold and few plants grow. It is quite different to other leopards – smaller and with a paler, thicker coat.

King of the jungle

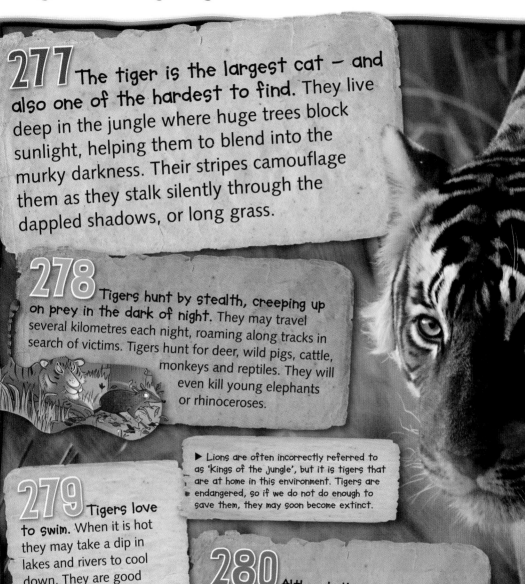

277 The tiger is the largest cat — and also one of the hardest to find. They live deep in the jungle where huge trees block sunlight, helping them to blend into the murky darkness. Their stripes camouflage them as they stalk silently through the dappled shadows, or long grass.

278 Tigers hunt by stealth, creeping up on prey in the dark of night. They may travel several kilometres each night, roaming along tracks in search of victims. Tigers hunt for deer, wild pigs, cattle, monkeys and reptiles. They will even kill young elephants or rhinoceroses.

▶ Lions are often incorrectly referred to as 'Kings of the jungle', but it is tigers that are at home in this environment. Tigers are endangered, so if we do not do enough to save them, they may soon become extinct.

279 Tigers love to swim. When it is hot they may take a dip in lakes and rivers to cool down. They are good swimmers and can make their way across large stretches of water.

280 Although they are powerful hunters, tigers may have to stalk 20 animals before they manage to catch just one. They normally kill once every five to six days and eat up to 40 kilograms of meat in one go! Tigers often return to a kill for several days until they have finished it, or scavengers (animals that eat food left by other animals) have carried it away.

281 Bengal tigers have a reputation as 'man-eaters'. Tigers don't usually eat people unless they are too sick or old to find other prey, but some tigers prefer the taste of human flesh. Between 1956 and 1983, more than 1500 people were killed by tigers in one region alone.

282 No two tigers have the same pattern of stripes. White tigers with black stripes are occasionally seen in the wild and are bred in zoos because they are popular with visitors. Although they don't look like their parents, these tigers are not different in any other way.

Jaws and claws

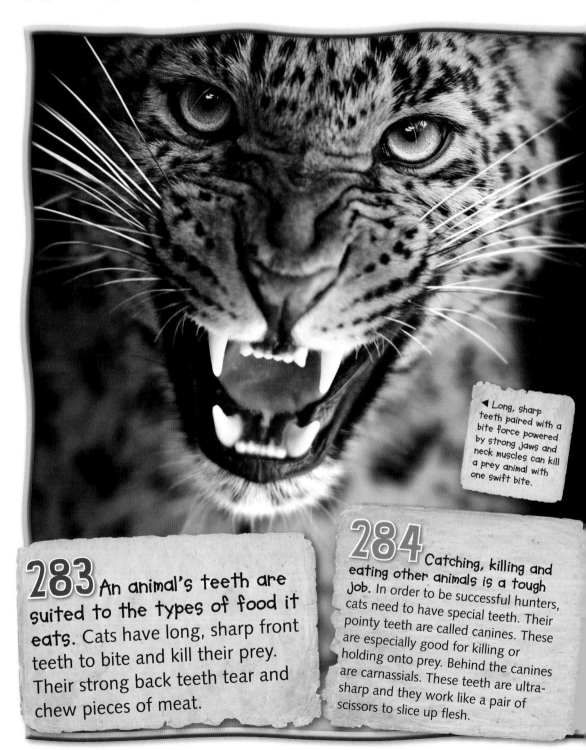

◄ Long, sharp teeth paired with a bite force powered by strong jaws and neck muscles can kill a prey animal with one swift bite.

283 An animal's teeth are suited to the types of food it eats. Cats have long, sharp front teeth to bite and kill their prey. Their strong back teeth tear and chew pieces of meat.

284 Catching, killing and eating other animals is a tough job. In order to be successful hunters, cats need to have special teeth. Their pointy teeth are called canines. These are especially good for killing or holding onto prey. Behind the canines are carnassials. These teeth are ultra-sharp and they work like a pair of scissors to slice up flesh.

286
A cat's tongue is very rough! This is because it is covered in hard spikes, or papillae. The scratchy surface is ideal for scraping meat off bones.

◀ Cats such as these lions can make their tongues into a scoop shape, which means that they can take big gulps of water when they are thirsty.

TRUE OR FALSE?

1. Cats can make their tongues into a scoop shape.
2. Cats have fur on the underside of their paws.
3. The spikes on a cat's tongue are called papillae.

Answers:
All are true

285
The paws of big cats and pet cats are very similar. All cats have paws that are armed with sharp, deadly daggers – claws. The bottom surface of each paw has soft pads that are surrounded by tufty fur to muffle the sound of every footstep.

▶ Each claw on this lynx's paw is curved and very sharp – a perfect tool for digging into its prey.

Spotted sprinter

287 A cheetah can run as fast as a car. Within 2 seconds of starting a chase, a cheetah can reach speeds of 75 kilometres an hour, and soon reaches a top speed of about 105 kilometres an hour – making it the world's fastest land animal. Cheetahs tire after about 30 seconds, so if its prey keeps out of reach for this amount of time, it may escape capture.

◀ A cheetah's body is perfectly adapted for sprinting. When it runs, only one paw will touch the ground at any one time.

288 This big cat lives in the grasslands and deserts of Africa and Middle East and Western Asia. Cheetahs do not often climb trees, as they have difficulty in getting down again. Cubs often hide in bushes so that they can surprise their prey. The word 'cheetah' means 'spotted wind' – the perfect name for this speedy sprinter.

▼ Cheetahs prefer wide open spaces where they can easily spot prey such as gazelles.

289 Like most of the big cats, cheetahs often live alone. Females live in an area called their 'home range', only leaving if food is scarce. When cubs leave their mothers they often stay together in small groups. Eventually the females go off to find their own home ranges, but the cubs may stay together and attack other cheetahs that come too close.

▼ Cheetahs kill antelopes by biting their throats, stopping them from getting any air.

290
A cheetah must rest before eating, or risk becoming dangerously over-heated. Cheetahs can spend a whole day eating if they go undisturbed by vultures or lions, which will steal the food if they can.

291
Cubs have thick tufts of long, pale fur on their heads, necks and shoulders. No one knows why – it might help to make them look bigger and stronger than they really are.

▶ Mothers keep their cubs hidden until they are old enough to start learning how to hunt.

292
There are usually between four and six cubs in one litter. Sadly, only one cub in every 20 lives to be an adult cheetah. The others are usually killed by lions or hyenas.

Sociable simba

293 **Lions are sociable animals.** They live in family groups called prides that normally include between four and six adults, all related, and their cubs. Large prides of perhaps 30 animals develop where there is plenty of food.

▲ Lionesses prepare an ambush by spreading out and circling their prey.

295 **The best time to hunt is early morning or evening.** Lions hunt zebra, wildebeest, impala and buffalo. A group of lionesses has been known to bring down an adult giraffe that was 6 metres tall!

294 **Unlike other big cats, male and female lions look very different.** They both have sandy-coloured fur that blends into sun-scorched grasslands, but the males have manes of darker hair on their heads and shoulders that make them look powerful and threatening.

► Lionesses give birth to a litter of between one and six cubs. The cubs stay with their mother for over two years.

296 Although it is unusual, lions do sometimes attack and eat humans. In the 1930s and 1940s, a lion family in Tanzania preferred human flesh to the normal lion diet of antelope. They killed nearly 1500 people in just 15 years.

297 Adult males only stay with their pride for a few years at a time. If a male wants to become the leader of another pride, it must fight the males and kill the cubs. This seems very cruel, but it does this to make the lionesses ready to have more cubs before it mates with them. The new leader then knows that all the cubs in the pride will be his own.

298 Few animals would dare to attack a healthy lion. When a lion has become old and weak, however, it may be easy prey for a band of hyenas. It is said that lions only fear hyenas – this is because they know they could end up in the bellies of several of them!

I DON'T BELIEVE IT!
Every cat's favourite pastime is napping. Lions spend almost 80 percent of their time sleeping, lying down or sitting doing nothing!

American athlete

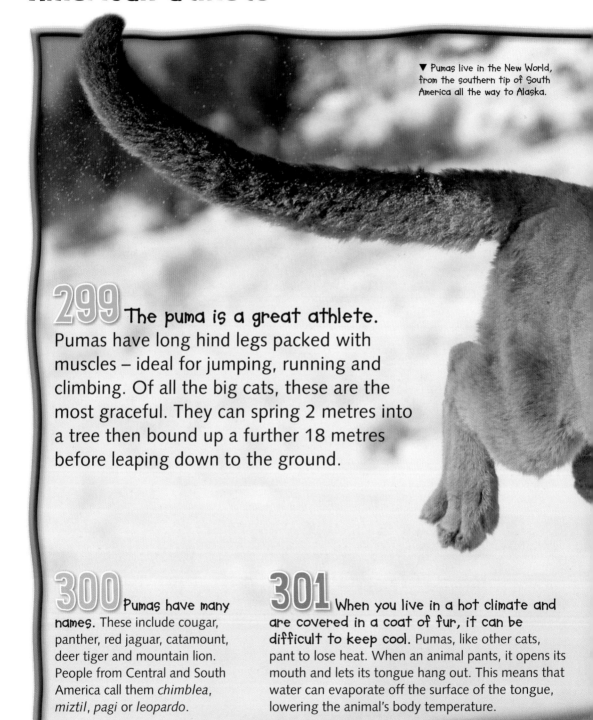

▼ Pumas live in the New World, from the southern tip of South America all the way to Alaska.

299 **The puma is a great athlete.** Pumas have long hind legs packed with muscles – ideal for jumping, running and climbing. Of all the big cats, these are the most graceful. They can spring 2 metres into a tree then bound up a further 18 metres before leaping down to the ground.

300 **Pumas have many names.** These include cougar, panther, red jaguar, catamount, deer tiger and mountain lion. People from Central and South America call them *chimblea*, *miztil*, *pagi* or *leopardo*.

301 **When you live in a hot climate and are covered in a coat of fur, it can be difficult to keep cool.** Pumas, like other cats, pant to lose heat. When an animal pants, it opens its mouth and lets its tongue hang out. This means that water can evaporate off the surface of the tongue, lowering the animal's body temperature.

302 Rabbits, mice, rats and hares are popular prey for pumas. They will also attack larger mammals, including deer, cattle and elks. In some places, humans have built houses in or near the pumas' natural habitat. This has resulted in people being attacked – even killed – by these wild animals. Now, people are beginning to realize that they have to respect the pumas' natural instincts and stay away from their territory.

303 Although pumas can kill porcupines, it is not an easy task. They need to flip the prickly creature onto its back before biting its soft belly. If the porcupine manages to spear the puma with one of its many spines, the wound may prove fatal.

I DON'T BELIEVE IT!
Pumas can't roar. Instead, they make an ear-piercing scream that scares both humans and animals alike, and gives it one of its many names: 'mountain-screamer'.

304 These big cats are highly skilled killers. They hunt by slowly creeping up on an unsuspecting victim. When ready, they pounce, knocking their prey to the ground in one sudden hit. A single, swift bite kills the puma's victim immediately.

A coat to die for

305 The jaguar is the owner of a beautiful fur coat — so beautiful that many people wanted to own it too. Although it is against the law to capture a jaguar for its skin, they are still hunted. Jaguars live in rainforests, often in areas where farmers are cutting back trees to grow crops. As jaguars' habitats continue to shrink, so will their numbers.

▶ Jaguars always live near water. They like swampy areas, or places that flood during wet seasons.

306 At first glance a jaguar looks like a leopard, but it is possible to tell them apart. A jaguar's head is bigger and rounder than a leopard's, with round ears not pointed ones. Its tail is quite a bit shorter than the leopard's and its shoulders are broad and packed with muscle.

307 Of all the big cats, jaguars are the most water-loving. They are strong swimmers and seem to enjoy bathing in rivers. Jaguars live in Central and South America but less than a hundred years ago, they were living as far north as California and Texas. They are the largest of South America's big cats.

308 Young jaguars climb trees where they hunt for birds and small mammals. As they grow bigger they become too heavy for the branches. Adults tend to stay on the ground, or in water, to hunt.

▲ Capybaras have webbed feet, and feed on grass and aquatic plants.

310 Jaguars hunt a wide range of animals including deer, tapirs, birds, fish and capybaras. Capybaras are the world's heaviest rodent and can measure up to 130 centimetres in length.

▼ This jaguar has caught a caiman (a small crocodile-like creature). They are ambush killers, and often despatch their prey with a single bite.

309 Jaguars' powerful jaws are so strong that they can crack open the hard shells of turtles and tortoises. These cats will even kill large animals, such as cattle and horses. It is their habit of killing cows that upsets many people who share the jaguars' territory. Cattle are very important to the farmers, who may poison or shoot jaguars that are killing their livestock.

Supercat

311 **Leopards can live close to humans but never be seen by them.** They live in Africa and as far east as Malaysia, China and Korea. Leopards hunt by night and sleep in the day. They are possibly the most common of all the big cats, but are rarely seen in the wild.

▼ There are probably more leopards in the wild than all the other big cats put together. This success has earned leopards the nickname 'supercat'.

312 **Leopards may sit in the branches of a tree, waiting patiently for their meal to come to them.** As their prey strolls past, the leopard drops from the branches and silently, quickly, kills its victim.

313 **Leopards nearly always hunt at night.** A leopard approaches its prey in absolute silence, making sure that it does not snap a twig or rustle leaves. With incredible control, it places its hind paws onto the exact places where its forepaws had safely rested. When it is within striking distance of its victim it will attack.

314 Leopards are not fussy eaters. They will eat dung beetles, frogs or birds if nothing better comes along. They prefer to hunt monkeys, pigs and antelopes.

315 Once a leopard has caught its meal, it does not want to lose it to passing scavengers such as hyenas or jackals. The leopard might climb up a tree, hauling its prey with it. It may choose to eat immediately or store the animal for later. Hiding food like this is called 'caching' (say 'cashing').

▼ Leopards have very strong front legs, so they can haul large prey into the safety of a tree's branches.

▼ Get close enough to a black panther and you'll see that its fur is spotted.

316 The name 'panther' is usually given to pumas, but it is also used for leopards that have black fur. Black panthers are not a different type of leopard – some cubs are simply born with black fur rather than the normal tawny-brown hide.

BEARS

317 **In the snowy lands surrounding the Arctic, bears used to be known as 'masters of the forest'.** Bears are some of the largest creatures to live on land and they have few natural enemies, except humans. Once they roamed many of the planet's forests, but now these magnificent animals face an uncertain future.

▶ Brown bears eat a lot of fish and often wait at rivers and waterfalls for salmon. They catch the fish in their powerful jaws, or hook them out of the water with their huge paws, but they have to be quick!

What is a bear?

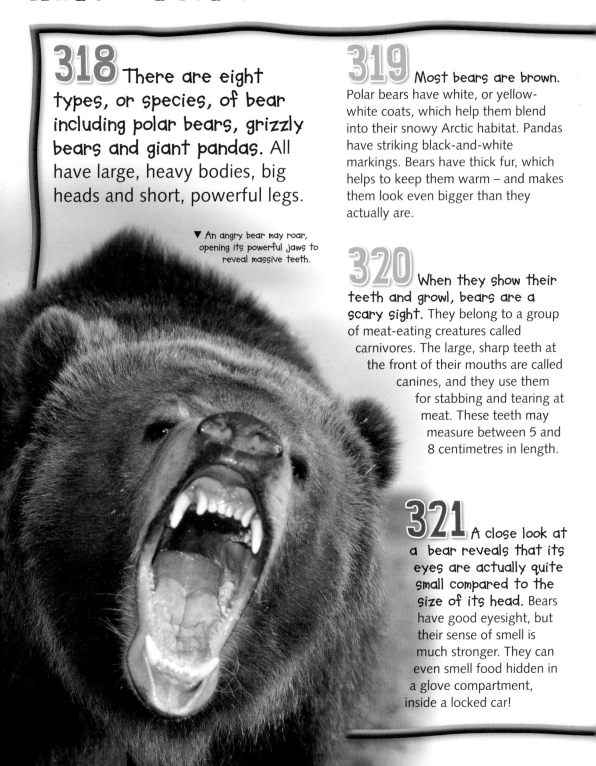

318 There are eight types, or species, of bear including polar bears, grizzly bears and giant pandas. All have large, heavy bodies, big heads and short, powerful legs.

▼ An angry bear may roar, opening its powerful jaws to reveal massive teeth.

319 Most bears are brown. Polar bears have white, or yellow-white coats, which help them blend into their snowy Arctic habitat. Pandas have striking black-and-white markings. Bears have thick fur, which helps to keep them warm – and makes them look even bigger than they actually are.

320 When they show their teeth and growl, bears are a scary sight. They belong to a group of meat-eating creatures called carnivores. The large, sharp teeth at the front of their mouths are called canines, and they use them for stabbing and tearing at meat. These teeth may measure between 5 and 8 centimetres in length.

321 A close look at a bear reveals that its eyes are actually quite small compared to the size of its head. Bears have good eyesight, but their sense of smell is much stronger. They can even smell food hidden in a glove compartment, inside a locked car!

▶ A bear's paws and claws are fearsome weapons, but they are most often used for digging up food such as roots. The Malayan sun bear's long, curved claws make it an excellent climber.

I DON'T BELIEVE IT!

Bears may look like they rely on strength rather than speed to survive, but don't be fooled. Brown bears can run at nearly 50 kilometres an hour — much faster than most humans.

322 Bears use their teeth to defend themselves in fights and to hunt other animals.

They have powerful paws to swipe at their attackers, and one blow can knock another animal to the ground. Their claws are long, knife-like, and reach up to 15 centimetres in length.

▼ A bear's skeleton helps to support its weight. The large skull protects the brain and the ribcage protects the internal organs.

Pelvis

Ribcage

Spine

Shoulder

Skull

Habits and homes

323 Today, most bear species are rare. They are still found in areas of the Arctic, the Americas, Europe and Asia, but once, bears lived in woodlands all over the world.

324 Bears can live in a variety of places, from the icy north to the hot forests of South-east Asia. Sloth bears can even live in dry scrubland as long as ants and honey are available. Despite their size, most bears can climb trees.

325 Although they are carnivores, bears often have to settle for a snack of leaves, roots and fruits. The polar bear eats only meat, because there are almost no plants in the Arctic, but other bears rely on plants for the bulk of their diet. Since plants don't contain as much energy-rich fat as meat, most bears have to spend lots of their time eating and searching for food.

▼ Bears like the sweet taste of ripe berries and feast on these in the autumn.

326 Bears are solitary animals — they prefer to live alone. Mothers and cubs make small families, but once they have grown, young bears head off on their own to face the world by themselves.

▲ Brown bears spend the winter sleeping in rocky caves lined with leaves and grass.

327 Bears make the most of the summer and autumn months, when there is more food around, to eat and gain weight. When winter comes, bears that live in cool or cold climates retreat to their dens and sleep through the worst weather. They need big stores of body fat to help them survive during this time as they may not eat for many months.

▶ A bear family stays close together for safety. The cubs are at risk of being hunted by other meat eaters, including other bears.

Black bears

328 Areas of North America and Canada are home to black bears. They live in mountains and forests, and despite being very shy, they sometimes stray into towns. They avoid brown bears, which also live in the American continent.

329 Most black bears are black, but some have brown or even white fur. Dark-furred black bears sometimes have lighter fur on their muzzles (noses) and chests. Their long, curved claws help them grip tree trunks when climbing trees.

TRUE OR FALSE?

1. A muzzle is the name given to some animals' long noses.
2. Black bears live in Europe.
3. 'Scavenge' means finding scraps and waste food.
4. A carnivore eats meat.

Answers:
1. True 2. False 3. True 4. True

330
These big bears need to eat plenty of food to keep their energy levels high. During the summer they mostly eat plants, but individual's diets depend on where they live, the time of year and what is available. Black bears rarely hunt other animals, although they eat insects such as beetles, and love honey.

331
Black bears are regarded as the most intelligent of all bears. Those that live near humans often use their sense of smell to locate rubbish bins. They find ways to break into the bins and rifle through piles of garbage. Black bears are often found in national parks where they wander into campsites in search of food, particularly at night.

◄ Black bears avoid humans, and if they see people they are much more likely to run away or climb up a tree than attack.

332
Thousands of black bears are killed by humans every year. Only one out of every ten black bears dies of natural causes. The others are all killed by hunters, or after being hit by cars. Yet black bears manage to survive and are not in danger of becoming extinct.

Polar bears

333 The polar bear is the biggest type of bear, and the largest meat-eating animal on Earth. These huge beasts have to fight to survive in one of the planet's bleakest places.

334 The Arctic is a snow-and-ice-covered region around the North Pole. Temperatures are record-breaking, dropping to an incredible −70°C and, unsurprisingly, very few living things are found there. Polar bears, however, manage to cope with howling winds, freezing snow blizzards and long winters.

I DON'T BELIEVE IT!

The word 'Arctic' comes from the Greek word 'Arkitos', which means country of the Great Bear. This doesn't refer to polar bears though, but to the Great Bear constellation, or pattern of stars, in the sky.

335 Polar bears are covered in a thick layer of white fur. This helps them to stay warm because it keeps in their body heat, and even absorbs some of the Sun's warming energy. Each hair is a colourless hollow tube which appears white when it reflects light. Some bears have yellow fur, especially in the summer when they spend less time in water and their coats get dirty.

336 Polar bears also have a layer of fat called blubber beneath the skin, which traps heat. This is where the bears store energy for the months when they may not be able to find food. The blubber may be up to 12 centimetres thick and is so effective at helping the bear stay warm that polar bears are more likely to get too hot than too cold!

337 Female polar bears spend the winter months in dens so their cubs can be born safely. A mother spends five or six months in the snug den with her cubs, while the bad winter weather rages outside. She doesn't eat or drink during all of this time, but survives on her body fat.

◀ The Arctic summer is short, so polar bears like to soak up the sunshine in between hunting trips. Young cubs stay close to their mother at all times.

Brown bears

338 The mighty brown bear is a massive, shaggy-haired beast that lives in the northern parts of the world. Long ago, brown bears were spread far and wide across the world, but now they are finding it difficult to survive in places where they come into contact with humans.

339 Brown bears are now mostly found in forests, mountains and scrubland, in remote places where few people roam. There are brown bears in Northern Europe, Siberia, Asia, Alaska, Canada and parts of the United States. Bears from different areas can look quite different from one another. They vary in colour from yellowish to almost black.

340 Kodiak bears are the largest of all brown bears, weighing up to 800 kilograms. They stand almost twice as high as a human. Their size is due to their diet – these big animals eat lots of fish, which is packed with healthy fats and proteins. Kodiak bears live on Kodiak Island, in Alaska, North America.

◄ A brown bear can reach 3 metres in length and normally weighs between 200 and 600 kilograms. They rub up against trees to scratch their backs.

342 Brown bears may be huge animals, but they can run with speed if they need to. When walking they appear slow and lumbering, but a scared bear can change pace very quickly – and run faster than most other animals.

341 Brown bears live in northern areas where it is very cold in winter, so they usually hibernate. Some types spend up to seven months in a den, but all bears wake up occasionally. When they wake they rearrange their bedding, clean themselves and return to sleep.

▶ Male bears are called boars and may sometimes fight one another using jaws, paws and claws.

343 Grizzlies are the famous brown bears of North America. They once roamed as far south as Mexico, but now they live in western Canada and Alaska. They get their name from the white hairs that grow in their brown coats, giving them a grizzled appearance.

Gone hunting

344 Grizzlies spend hours wading in water, or standing on a river's edge watching and waiting for salmon. During the summer and autumn, salmon swim upstream to lay their eggs, and as the fish swim past, the bears pounce on them.

345 With a single blow from its large paw, a bear can easily stun a fish. Grizzlies can also catch their prey in their mouths, delivering a quick and fatal bite with their enormous teeth. Grizzlies are good swimmers, and will even dive underwater to catch salmon swimming past them.

▲ Grizzlies usually hunt and kill their prey, but they will also eat animal remains that have been abandoned by other hunters.

346 From berries, shoots and roots to insects, fish and small mammals, grizzlies will eat almost anything. Sometimes they hunt living animals, especially young elks or caribou deer. They also eat carrion – the dead remains of animals killed by other predators (hunters) – such as wolves, coyotes and other bears.

◀ A grizzly chases a salmon through the water. Salmon are highly nutritious, so brown bears that hunt them often grow bigger than other brown bears.

▼ Grizzlies stand and wait for salmon to leap out of the water. Like other brown bears, they have distinctive humps on their shoulders.

348 Grizzlies inspired the first teddy bear, which appeared around 100 years ago. Teddies were named after an American president called Theodore 'Teddy' Roosevelt, who refused to shoot a grizzly on a hunting trip. The story was in a newspaper and a toyshop owner decided to make a stuffed bear – and called it a teddy.

347 Grizzlies may travel a long way in search of food, but they usually return to their territory. Bears are sometimes trapped and moved to other areas by scientists and wildlife managers to keep them away from humans, but a few have been able to find their way home – up to 200 kilometres away. No one knows how they do this, but their great sense of smell may help.

MY HOME

Do you know where you live? Ask a grown up to help you find your street on a map of your area, and then find your school. Can you trace the route home from your school, following the roads? Then use a big atlas and find your country on a map of the world.

Bear behaviour

349 Most bears are shy creatures and prefer to avoid coming into contact with humans. Mother bears, however, will attack any person or animal that comes too close to her cubs.

▶ When bears live near humans, they lose their fear of them and may even start to scavenge rubbish and other food.

350 Angry bears give warning signs that they may attack. These include making huffing noises, beating the ground with their paws or even making short charges. They may start growling, and their ears lie flat to their heads. Some bears do attack humans for food, but this is extremely rare – and they don't give any warning signs first. Running away from a bear just encourages them to start chasing.

CAUTION

ACTIVE BEARS IN AREA

PLEASE USE CAUTION WHILE WALKING:

- CARRY A BELL
- MAKE NOISE
- BE ALERT

351 Many grizzlies have learnt that they will find a free lunch wherever there are people. If grizzlies overcome their fear of humans they can become very dangerous. Once they have found a place where they can get food, they will return to it again and again.

◀ Being 'bear aware' can be a life-saver in some parts of the world. Bears are most dangerous when startled, so making plenty of noise when you're hiking in bear territory is one way of preventing an attack.

▼ A biologist weighs a sedated polar bear cub as part of a health check. Finding out how this species is doing gives us clues to the health of the whole Arctic marine ecosystem.

352 **Dogs are being used in the Canadian Rocky Mountains to help train grizzlies to stay away from humans.** Troublesome bears that wander close to areas where there are lots of people are sedated with drugs that send them to sleep. When they wake up, the dogs bark and growl at them, chasing them away until they reach the safety of the woodlands. The bears quickly learn to stay away from houses!

353 **American black bears are often feared by campers, but they rarely attack people.** In fact bears have much more reason to fear humans than we have to fear them. Around 30 to 40 people have been killed by black bears in the United States in the last 100 years, but 30,000 of these beautiful creatures are killed by humans every year.

BEAR SCARE!

The advice if you see a bear up close is to slowly back away, watching it all the time. If the bear follows you, stand and wave your arms around while shouting loudly. The idea is to frighten the bear away, so you have to look as mean and angry as you can! Practise your angry face and shouting – you'll probably find it quite easy!

Bear myths and legends

354 Bears are seen as mighty, magical and majestic creatures in many cultures. They feature in folk tales and legends throughout the world, and are feared and respected in equal amounts.

355 Bears are sometimes thought of as powerful spirits that can influence peoples' lives. Long ago, people in northern countries feared a bear spirit could control other animals, and even take them away if they upset him.

356 Berserkirs were Viking warriors who dressed themselves in bear skins and worked themselves into a trance before battle. In this state, they were wild and fearless and dangerous to anyone who got in their way. This is where the word 'berserk' comes from.

◀ Viking Berserkir warriors rushed madly into battle, wearing bear skins over their chain mail armour.

I DON'T BELIEVE IT!

Bears inspire people who want to be as strong as they are, so some sports teams are named after them. The Chicago Bears, for example, are an American football team and the Memphis Grizzlies are basketball players.

◀ A Danish legend tells of a bear that was the king's ancestor. The bear was killed by dogs, but survives in folk tales.

357 A Danish story describes how a bear and a beautiful woman fell in love. The bear cared for her by stealing food from farms, until one day, farmers used dogs and spears to kill him. The woman later gave birth to a boy that looked normal, but was as strong and brave as a bear, who became the ancestor of the kings of Denmark.

▼ A giant armoured bear, called Iorek, features in the 2008 movie *The Golden Compass*, which is based on the book *Northern Lights*, by Philip Pullman.

358 The Samoyed and Lapps are tribes of people who live close to the North Pole. Like other people who share bear habitats, they used to believe that, with the use of magic, humans could turn themselves into bears. Brave warriors were often thought to have taken on the spirits of bears as they fought.

Index

Entries in **bold** refer to main subject entries. Entries in *italics* refer to illustrations

A

accipiters 120
adders 97
African boomslang 92
African hunting dog 14, 15, *15*
African rock python *81*
Alaska 150, 151
alligators **16–17**, *16*, *17*
American black bear **146–147**, *146–147*, 155
amphisbaenians 80
anacondas *8*, *78*
anemones 54, 55, 72, *72*
anthill python 101
antivenom 75, 76, 95
ants **34–35**, 40, 58, 59, *59*
arachnids 25
Arctic 140, 142, 144, 148, *149*
Asia 144, 150
Asian cobra 75
Asian giant hornet 59
asps 97
assassin bug 58, *58*
auger shell 57
Australian redback spider 61

B

baboons 12
bald eagle **115**, *115*
ball python 100, *100*
barn owl *109*
barracuda 28, *28*
beaded lizard 68
beaked sea snake 95
bearded dragon lizard 69
bee-eater bird 73, *73*
bees 35, *35*, 46, 52, 58, *58*, 76, *76*
Bengal tigers 127
bills *105*, **108**, 122
birth 101
black kite 116, *116*
black mamba *48*, 87, 95, *95*
black panther 139
black vulture *109*
black widow spider 24, *24*, 40, *48–49*, 61
blubber 149
blue jeans frog *22*
blue shark 30
blue spotted stingray *67*
blue-capped ifrita *45*
blue-ringed octopus 29, *29*, 43, 51, **56–57**, *57*, 75
boars *151*
boas *8–9*, *9*, 89, 91, 98, **100–101**
bodies 80, 81, 82, 84, 86, *87*, 91, 97, 99, *99*
body fat 145, 149
bombardier beetle 40, *40–41*
bonnethead shark *73*
box jellyfish 28, *28*, 51, 55, *74*, 75
Brazilian wandering spider 60

brown bears *140*, *144*, *145*, 146, **150–151**, *150*, *152*, *153*, *154*
see also grizzly bear, Kodiak bear
brown recluse spider 51
buffalo 18
bull shark 30
bullet ant 59, *59*
burrowing snakes 83
bush viper 97
bushmaster viper 97
Buteos *117*
buzzards *102–103*, **117**, *117*

C

caching 139
caiman *137*
camouflage 27, *32*, 85, *85*, 100, *100*, 126
Canada 144, 150, 151, 155
Cape porcupine *26*
capybara 137, *137*
carnivores **8–9**, 142, 144
carrion 102, 152
caterpillars *42–43*, 49, 52, *52*
cellar spider *49*
centipedes 53, **62–63**, *63*
chameleon 27
cheetahs 130–131
chicks *103*, *123*
children's python 90
chimp 12, *12–13*
claws 11, *11*, 129, *129*, 143, *143*, 146, 151
climbing 143, 144, *147*
clownfish 72
cnidocytes 54, *54*
coachwhip snake 88
cobalt blue tarantula spider *40*
cobras 41, 47, *47*, 75, 92, 94, 95, **96–97**, *96*
colours *82*, **84–85**, *84*, 91, *91*, *100*
colubrids 98
common black hawk *121*
common buzzard *117*
common krait 95
cone shells 33, *33*, 56, *56*, 77, *77*
constrictor snakes 9, *78*, **98–99**, 100–101, *100*, *101*
Cooper's hawk **121**
copperhead 97
coral 54, 55, *55*
coral snake 27, 83, 84, 94, 96
cougar 134
cowfish 45
coyote 14, 15
crocodiles *6–7*, **16–17**, *16*, *17*
crown-of-thorns starfish 52, 64, *64*
Cuban solenodon 71, *71*
cubs 130, *131*, 132, *132*, 139, 145, 149, *149*, 154, *154*
cuttlefish 57, *57*

D

deadly nightshade 44
death adder 91
death cap mushroom *44*

death stalker scorpion 63, 75, *75*
defence 6, **26–27**, 41, 44, **46–47**
Denmark 157
dens 145, 149, 151
deserts 100
diadema sea urchin 65
diet 144, 150
digestion 81, 90, 94, 99, *99*
diseases 25, 34, **36–37**
dog bear *see* Malayan sun bear
dog family **14–15**
dogfish shark 66, *66*
domestic cats 124
duck-billed platypus 70, *70–71*, *71*

E

eagle owl 122, *123*
eagles 11, 102, *104*, 105, 107, *107*, 108, *108*, 110, 111, *113*, *113*, **114–115**, *114*, *115*
ears 154
echinoderms **64–65**
egg-eating snake 90, *90*
eggs 90, 101, 123
Egyptian vulture *105*
elapids 96
electric eel 27
Eleonora's falcon *118*
elephants 11, 19, *19*
elf owl 123
emerald tree boa 101, *101*
emperor scorpion 62, *62*
Eurasian eagle owl 122, 123
Eurasian sparrowhawk **121**, *121*
Europe 144, 150
extinction 126, 147
eyelash viper 53, 89, 93, *93*, 94
eyes 83, *83*, 88, 89, *89*, *104*, *104*, 122, *122*, 142

F

falcons *105*, 108, **118–119**, *118*, *119*
fangs 53, 92, *92*, 93, *93*, 94, 95, 96, 97
feathers 104, *108*, 122
fighting 143, *151*
Finding Nemo (film) 55
fire coral 55, *55*
fire salamander 21, *21*, **46–47**
fire urchin 65, *65*
fish 41, *41*, 43, *43*, 45, 46, 52, **66–67**, 66, 67, 73, *73*, 74, 75, 140, 144, 150, 152
fleas 36
flight *104*, **106–107**, *106*
flower urchin 65
fly agaric toadstool *44*
folk tales 156, *157*
food 81, **90–91**, 92, 94
foraging 144
forest 140, 144, 146, 150
frogs **22–23**, 45, *45*
funnel web spider 25, *25*
fur 142, 146, 149
  cheetah 131
  jaguar 136
  leopard 139
  puma 134
  snow leopard *124–125*

G

gaboon viper 85, *85*
Gila monster 21, *21*, 46, **68–69**, *68–69*
Golden Compass, The (film) 157
golden eagle *104*, *107*, 108, *108*, **114**
gorillas 12, 13
goshawk 120, *120–121*
great horned owl *122*
great white shark 30, *30*
green tree python 101, *101*
grey reef shark 31
grizzly bear *142*, *142*, 151, **152–153**, *152*, *153*, *154*, 155
gyrfalcon *105*, 118, **119**, *119*

H

habitat
  bears 142, **144–145**, 157
  boas and pythons 100
  destruction of 136, 137
  jaguar 136, 137
  lion 132
  puma 134, 135
hammerhead shark 73, *73*
harpy eagle **115**, *115*
harriers 121
hawks 108, 117, **120–121**, *121*
hen harrier 121
hibernation 145, *145*, 151
hippopotamus 18, *18–19*
hobbies 106
honey 144, 147
honey buzzard 117
hornets 58, 59, *59*
house spider 49
housefly *34*
huntsman spider 72

I

ice 148
iguanas 69
inland taipan snake 75, *75*
insects **34–35**, **58–59**, *58*, *59*, 147
Irukandji jellyfish 55, *55*

J

jack fish 45
Jacobson's organ 88, *88*
jaguars 134, **136–137**
jaws 81, 90, 91, **92–93**, *93*, 99, 140, 142, 151
jellyfish 28, *28*, 51, 54, *54*, 55, *55*, *74*, 75
jumping spider 61
jungle cats 126

K

Kenyan sand boa *100*
keratin 82
kestrels 106, *106*, 119, *119*
killer bee 35
killer whale 8
king cobra 91, 95
kingsnake 73, *90*, 98
kites 110, *110*, **116**, *116*
Kodiak bear 150
Komodo dragon 20, *20*, 69, *69*, 81, *81*

L

ladybirds 46
lammergeier 111, *111*
lancehead snake 51
Lapps 157
leaf-nosed snake *85*
legends **156–157**, *157*
leopards *128*, 138–139
 snow *124–125*
 spots 136
lesser kestrel *119*
lesser spotted eagle 110
lesser weeverfish 41, *41*
lionfish 33, *46*
lions *27*, *129*, 132–133
 cubs 132
 mountain 134
 prides 132–133
lizards **20–21**, 46, **68–69**, *68*, *69*, 80, *80*, 81, *81*
locusts 34, 35
long-legged centipede *63*
lynx *129*

M

malaria 37, *37*
Malayan sun bear *143*
mambas 85
 black *48*, 87, 95, *95*
mandrill *10*
marine toad 44, *44*
medicines 95
Mexican cantil *91*
Mexico 151
migration 118
milking venom 76, *76*
mimicry *27*
molluscs **56–57**, *56*, *57*
mongoose *47*, 73
monkshood *44*
moon moth caterpillar *42–43*
mosquito 37, *37*
moulting 83
mountain lion 134
movement **86–87**
mushroom, death cap *44*
muzzle 146
myths **156–157**

N

Natal green snake *89*
national parks 147
needle-spined sea urchin 65
nests *103*, 123, *123*
New Zealand katipo spider 61
night adder *97*
North America 144, 146, 150, 151, 153
North Pole 148, 157
Northern Lights (book) 157

O

octopus 29, *29*, *56–57*, 57
oilfish 45
orca *see* killer whale
oriental whip snake *89*
osprey *109*, **110**, *110–111*
owls 108, *108–109*, 109, **122–123**, *122*, *123*

P

palm viper *97*
palm-nut vulture 110
pandas 142
panther, black 139, *139*
panting 134
paradise tree snake *87*
parasites **36–37**
Parotostigmus centipede *63*
patterns **84–85**, 100, 127
paws 129, 140, 143, *143*, 151, 152, 154
pellets **123**, *123*
pelvis *143*
peregrine falcon **118**, *118*
piranha 9, *9*
pit viper 89, *97*
pitohui birds 45
plague 36, *36*
plants 44, *44*
poison 80, 84, 90, 91, 92, *92*, *93*, **94–95**, *95*, 96
poison-dart frogs 22, **22–23**, 45, *45*
polar bear 142, *143*, 144, **148–149**, *148–149*
porcupine 26
porcupinefish *43*
Portuguese man o' war 29, *54*
predators 84, 85, 96, 152
prides 132, 133
primates **12–13**
puff adder *93*, 97
pufferfish 26, *26*, 43, *43*, 45
Pullman, Philip 157
pumas 134–135
pythons 80, 89, 90, 91, 98, **100–101**

Q

queen snake 90

R

rainbow boa *84*
rainforests 85, 101, 136
rat snake 98
rats 36
rattlesnakes *47*, 51, 93, 97
red jaguar 134
red kite **116**, *116*
red-banded digger wasp 49, *49*
red-tailed hawk *121*
redback spider 46, *46*
reptiles **80–81**
research 49, **76–77**
rhinoceroses 19
ribs 87, 91, 96, *143*
ring-necked snake *84–85*, 85
roaring 135
Roosevelt, Theodore 'Teddy' 153
running 134
Russell's viper 75, 95

S

saker falcon *118*
salmon *140*, 152, *152*, 153
Samoyed 157
sand boa 100, *100*
saw-scaled viper 97

scales 80, **82–83**, *82*, *83*, 84, *84*, 97
scavenging *154*
Scolopendra gigantea centipede 63
scorpion fish 66, *66*
scorpions 10, 25, 52, **62–63**, *62*, 75, *75*
scutes 82, *86*
sea cucumber 65, *65*
sea snail 56
sea snakes 33, 51, 87, 94, 96
sea urchins 52, 64, 65, *65*
sea wasp 28
secretary bird 73, *73*, **112–113**, *112*
self-defence *see* defence
senses **88–89**, 104, 105, 108
 smell 142, 147, 153
sharks **30–31**, 66, *66*, 73, *73*
sharp-shinned hawk 120
short-toed eagle 113, *113*
shoulders, bear *143*, 153
shrews 70
shrimp 72, *72*
Siberia 150
sidewinding snakes 86, *86*
skeleton
 bird of prey *106*
 bear *143*
skin, snake 80, **82–83**, *82*, *83*, 89, 96
skulls
 snake 92, *93*
 bear *143*
sloth bear 144
small cats 124
snail kite 110, *110*
snake-charming 96
snow leopard *124–125*
solenodon 71, *71*
South-east Asia 144
sparrowhawk 120, 121, *121*
spiders **24–25**, *38–39*, 40, *40*, 46, *46*, 48, 49, *49*, 51, 53, **60–61**, *60*, *61*, 72, 75
spines 52, *52*, **64–65**, *65*, 66
spitting cobra 41, 96, **96–97**
spurs 71
squid 57
stargazer fish 67, *67*
stingray 10, *29*, 67, *67*
stings 52, *52*, 55, 59, 62
stonefish 32, *32*, 74, 75
sunbeam snake 84, 98
surgeon fish 66
Swainson's hawk 117
swallow-tailed kite 116, *116*
swimming 126, 136, 152
Sydney funnel-web spider *38–39*, 61, *61*, 75
symbiosis 72

T

talons 104, *105*, **108–109**, *108*, *109*, 122
tapeworms 37
tarantulas 24, 40, *41*, 60
tawny owl *108–109*, 109, *123*
teddy bears 153

teeth **92–93**, 98, *98*, 128, *128*, 137, 142, *142*, 143, 152
territory 153, *154*
thermals 107, *107*, *114*
thirst snake 90
ticks 25
tigers **126–127**
tongue 81, 88, *88*, 129, 134
tortoises 27
trapping 153
tree snakes 86, *86*, 87, 88
tsetse fly 37
tuatara 80
turkey vulture 105
tusks 11, 19

U

United States 150, 155

V

vampire bats 8, *8*
velvet ant 47
Vikings 156, *156*
vine snakes 89
vipers 85, 86, 89, *89*, 91, 92, *93*, 94, *94*, 95, **96–97**
vultures 102, 105, *105*, 107, *109*, 110

W

warning displays **46–47**
warriors 156, *156*, 157
wart snake 83
wasps 46, 47, 49, *49*, 52, *52*, 58, 59
white-tailed eagle *105*, 111
wings 105, 106, 107
winter 145, 148, 149, 151
wolves 14, *14*
woodlands 144, 155
woolly bear caterpillar 52, *52*
worms 37

Z

zoos 127

Acknowledgements

The publishers would like to thank the following sources for the use of their photographs:
Key: t = top, b = bottom, l = left, r = right, c = centre, bg = background, m = main

Alamy 41 Paulo Oliveira; 64 imagebroker; 78–79 age footstock; 84–85 Jack Goldfarb/Design Pics Inc; 108–109 A & J Visage; 117 blickwinkel; 148–149(m) Juniors Bildarchiv GmbH; 153(m) Wayne Johnson/Design Pics Inc; 157(br) Colombe de Meurin/Collection Christophel

Ardea 44(b) Jean Paul Ferrero; 83(cr) John Cancalosi; 92 Chris Harvey/Ardea.com

Australian Reptile Park (www.reptilepark.com.au) 76(t)

Deposit Photos 128 kyslynskyy

Diomedia 61(tr) F1online RM/F. Rauschenbach

Dreamstime 83(tr) Picstudio; 89(top inset) Sharkegg

FLPA 23 Mark Moffett/Minden Pictures; 28(tr) Kelvin Aitken/Biosphoto; 49(tr) Rene Krekels/Minden Pictures; 60(b) James Christensen/Minden Pictures; 65(t and b) Fred Bavendam/Minden Pictures; 67(t) R. Dirscherl; 69(t) Gerry Ellis/Minden Pictures; 82(l) Michael & Patricia Fogden/Minden Pictures; 115 Imagebroker, Bernd Zoller; 119 Ramon Navarro/Minden Pictures; 123 Roger Tidman; 126–127(m) Jami Tarris/Minden Pictures; 129(b) Christian Heinrich/Imagebroker; 137(b) Patrick Fagot; 139(br) Alain Compost/Biosphoto; 144(bg) Michio Hoshino/Minden Pictures; 145(b) Derek Middleton; 150(bg) Mike Lane; 152(tr) Sumio Harada/Minden Pictures, (bl) Frans Lanting; 154(tr) Yva Momatiuk & John Eastcott/Minden Pictures

Fotolia 11 Photomac; 17 Eric Gevaert; 24 Reiner Weidemann; 80(panel. clockwise from tr) Becky Stares, Vatikaki, Eric Gevaert, Ralf Broskuar

Getty 36 John Downer/Oxford Scientific; 53(tl) David A. Northcott/Corbis Documentary; 54–55(bg) Wolfgang Poelzer/WaterFrame; 59(tr) Alastair Macewen/Oxford Scientific; 72(b) David Fleet Visuals Unlimited; 81(b) Werner Bollmann/Oxford Scientific; 90–91(tc) John Cancalosi/age fotostock; 91 Carol Farneti Foster/Photodisc; 94 David A. Northcott/Corbis Documentary; 96–97 Digital Vision; 110(bl) Arthur Morris/Corbis Documentary; 120–121 W.Perry Conway/Corbis; 142(bl) Renee Lynn/Corbis/VCG/Corbis Documentary

iStock 63(c) Laurie Knight; 82(tr) Mark Kostich; 84(bl) Seth Ames; 86(tl) lara seregni; 89(b) Mark Kostich; 95(cr) Mark Kostich/iStockphoto.com; 100(br) Eric Isselée; 154(bl)

Movie Store Collection 55(c) Walt Disney Pictures, Pixar Animation Studios, Disney Enterprises

Nature Picture Library 15 Bruce Davidson; 42–43 Ingo Arndt; 48 Lynn M. Stone; 66(b) Wild Wonders of Europe/Banfi; 73(b) Wild Wonders of Europe/Varesvu; 83(bl) Visuals Unlimited; 87(b) Tim MacMillan/John Downer Pr; 102–103 Wild Wonders of Europe/Nill/; 107 Markus Varesvuo; 110–111 Markus Varesvuo; 113 Luis Quinta; 155 Suzi Eszterhas

Oceanwide Images 56–57 Gary Bell

Photoshot 21 Daniel Heuclin/NHPA/Avalon; 35 MartinHarvey/NHPA/Avalon; 38–39 Ken Griffiths/NHPA; 42(bl), 58 & 76(c) Anthony Bannister/NHPA; 45(br) Bruce Beehler/NHPA; 51 Daniel Heuclin/NHPA; 63(b) A.N.T./NHPA; 76(cr) NHPA; 100(tl) Daniel Heuclin; 116 Jordi Bas Casas

Science Photo Library 50 Alan Sirulnikoff; 53(br) B. Boissonnet; 76 Louise Murray; 77(b) Volker Steger

Shutterstock endpapers worldswildlifewonders; 1 kyslynskahal; 2–3 Richard J Ashcroft; 4–5 Ronnie Howard; 44–45(border) Arena Creative; 44(panel: clockwise from top left) Pertusinas, picturepartners, Jens Ottoson; 46 Rich Carey; 48(c) photobar; 49(b) vblinov; 50–51(bg) Peter Gudella; 52(tr) David Kelly, (bl) Anton Harder, (br) Anobi; 55(bl) Anna segeren; 57(br) John A. Anderson; 58(bl) kurt_G; 63(t) Audrey Snider-Bell; 65(c) almond; 69(br) Janelle Lugge; 74 bernd.neeser; 74–75 (tl, bl, tr, br) R-studio; 76(b) markrhiggins; 124–125 Karen Kane – Alberta, Canada; 129(t) Hedrus; 130(b) Stuart G Porter; 131(tl) Ryan M. Bolton, (r) Alan Jeffery; 132(t) By Braam Collins; 134–135 Dennis W Donohue; 136 Kris Wiktor; 137(t) Vadim Petrakov; 138–139(m) Martin Prochazkacz; 139(r) Ewan Chesser

All other photographs are from: DigitalSTOCK, digitalvision, John Foxx, PhotoAlto, PhotoDisc, PhotoEssentials, PhotoPro, Stockbyte

Front cover artwork Stuart Jackson-Carter

All other artworks are from the Miles Kelly Artwork Bank

Every effort has been made to acknowledge the source and copyright holder of each picture.
Miles Kelly Publishing apologizes for any unintentional errors or omissions.